UNIVERSITY OF NOTRE DAME
WARD-PHILLIPS LECTURE IN
ENGLISH LANGUAGE AND LITERATURE
Volume 2

The Form of Victorian Fiction

J. Hillis Miller

THE
FORM OF
VICTORIAN FICTION

Thackeray, Dickens, Trollope,
George Eliot, Meredith, and Hardy

Notre Dame & London
UNIVERSITY OF NOTRE DAME PRESS

Grateful acknowledgment is herewith made to the following for permission to quote from the books listed below.

To Macmillan & Co. Ltd. and The Trustees of the Hardy Estate for permission to quote from *Desperate Remedies* by Thomas Hardy.

To Macmillan & Co. Ltd., The Trustees of the Hardy Estate, and St. Martin's Press for permission to quote from *A Pair of Blue Eyes* and *Far From the Madding Crowd* by Thomas Hardy, and for permission to quote from *The Life of Thomas Hardy: 1840–1928* by Florence Emily Hardy (London: Macmillan; New York: St. Martin's Press, 1965. Copyright © Macmillan & Co. Ltd., 1962).

To Macmillan & Co. Ltd., The Trustees of the Hardy Estate, and The Macmillan Company for permission to quote from *The Mayor of Casterbridge* by Thomas Hardy.

FOR
MY MOTHER

FOREWORD

This book is made up of four lectures given at the University of Notre Dame on April 10, 11, 13, and 14, 1967, by J. Hillis Miller, Professor of English and Chairman of the Department at the Johns Hopkins University. They were the second of an annual series, the Ward-Phillips Lectures in English Language and Literature, established in 1966 under the auspices of the Department of English.

The series is named in honor of two deceased members of the English faculty, Reverend Leo L. Ward, C.S.C., and Professor Charles Phillips, both of whom were writers as well as teachers. Father Ward's stories of farm life in his native southern Indiana appeared in such distinguished "little magazines" as the *Midland* and have since been collected in the posthumously published volume, *Men in the Field*. Professor Phillips published several books, including collections of poems and critical essays, plays, and a biography of Paderewski.

However, these two men are remembered chiefly

for what they did as teachers to advance the study of letters among their students and colleagues. After a brief career of only nine years at Notre Dame, Professor Phillips, at the time of his death in 1933, had earned a place as one of the great teachers in the history of the University. He had also taken an important part in establishing the University Theater. Father Ward began teaching English at Notre Dame in 1929, and as head of the department from 1936 until his death in 1953, he did much to give our department its distinctive, creative character.

We are proud to present this publication by the University Press of Professor Miller's lectures on *The Form of Victorian Fiction* which maintains the same high level of distinction as those of the late Professor Frederick Hoffman, our first Ward-Phillips Lecturer.

Ernest Sandeen, *Chairman*
Department of English
University of Notre Dame

PREFACE

TAKING "FORM" AS A TERM FOR THE INNER STRUC-
turing principles of a work rather than for its external shape, this book discusses some aspects of form
in Victorian fiction. Each of the great Victorian
novels is unique and can be completely understood
only on its own terms. Nevertheless, each embodies
in its own way a period form and period conventions
as distinctive as those of romanesque or Gothic
architecture. Each novel contributes to the exploration of a spiritual and cultural situation peculiar to
one time and place, although this situation is experienced differently by each writer of the age. I have
tried to add to the understanding of Victorian England by interpretation of the literary form used by
many of its greatest writers.

William Makepeace Thackeray (1811–1863),
Charles Dickens (1812–1870), Anthony Trollope
(1815–1882), George Eliot (1819–1880), George
Meredith (1828–1909), and Thomas Hardy (1840–
1928), are major novelists whom any description

of form in Victorian fiction must take into account. I have centered this analysis on characteristic master-works by each of these: Thackeray's *Vanity Fair* and *Henry Esmond;* Dickens' *Oliver Twist* and *Our Mutual Friend;* Trollope's *Ayala's Angel;* George Eliot's *Adam Bede* and *Middlemarch;* Meredith's *The Egoist;* Hardy's *A Pair of Blue Eyes.*

Three questions are crucial to Victorian fiction: the question of time, the question of interpersonal relations, and the question of realism. The four chapters of this book are organized around a discussion of these questions in their relations to one another. A novel, it is true, is as much as any other work of literature the expression of the way a single consciousness, that of its author, has appropriated his world. One aim of the criticism of fiction is identification of the unique flavor of that consciousness in any given case. In a novel, however, the expression of this special quality, the peculiar Dickensian, Trollopian, or Meredithian note, is mediated, indirect. It is to be approached only by way of the interaction of the imaginary minds of the narrator and his characters as they are related within the horizon opened by time in the novel. My goal in this book has been to suggest ways for reaching the former by interpretation of its incarnation in the latter.

The date of each novel is given the first time it is mentioned in the text. When citations are made I have provided chapter and book numbers as well as page numbers for ·the convenience of readers who may be using different editions of the novels. When a number of quotations are made from the same text, the first is identified in a footnote, and subsequent references are given in parentheses after the quotations.

This book is a revised and somewhat expanded form of the second annual Ward-Phillips Lectures given at the University of Notre Dame in April of 1967. The week I spent at Notre Dame was extremely pleasant, and I wish to thank the University and the Department of English for many courtesies. My audience was most intelligent and attentive, and the final book is better for their response. I am especially grateful for the unfailing kindnesses and hospitalities of Professor and Mrs. Ernest Sandeen and Professor Joseph Duffy. I wish also to acknowledge the efficient help in the preparation of this book of Miss Emily M. Schossberger and Miss Theresa Lapenta of the University of Notre Dame Press. Finally, I wish to thank the John Simon Guggenheim Memorial Foundation for the Fellowship which gave me time to work out the ideas in this book.

J. Hillis Miller
Bayside, Maine
August 22, 1967

CONTENTS

TIME AND INTERSUBJECTIVITY

1

OUR MUTUAL FRIEND (1864–1865), OR THE LAST
Chronicle of Barset (1866–1867), or *Middlemarch* (1871–1872), or *The Mayor of Casterbridge*
(1886), is, like any other work of literature, made
exclusively of words. In this sense it may be said to
designate an imaginary or mental world. The words
of a novel objectify the mind of an author and make
that mind available to others. An analogy may be
found for this in everyday life. The hidden consciousness of each person we meet is incarnated in
his body, in his gestures, his facial expression, his
speech. This presence in the world opens the other
person to our spontaneous and unreflecting comprehension. The writing of a novel is also a gesture,
and this is its primary reality. It brings into visibil-
ity what its author is. A man is what he does, and
this is as true for the writing of a novel as for any
other action. Every page of *Oliver Twist* (1837–
1839), or *David Copperfield* (1849–1850), expresses something more than any theme or story or
dramatization of character. It expresses the unique
quality of Dickens' mind. The fact that a novel is
made of words means that it is also a form of consciousness. The reading or criticism of Victorian

1

fiction is therefore, like any other reading or criticism, to be defined as consciousness of the consciousness of another. Through the act of reading the reader tries to identify himself with another mind and to reexperience from the inside the feelings and thoughts of that mind. Reading a novel is a form of intersubjectivity.

A novel, however, differs from many other forms of literature, lyric poetry for instance, in that the mind which its words express is not a single meditating or perceiving consciousness, not a solitary mind exploring itself or exploring its relations to objects outside itself—trees, flowers, mountains, and clouds. A novel is a structure of interpenetrating minds, the mind of the narrator as he beholds or enters into the characters, the minds of the characters as they behold or know one another. Not isolated consciousness, not consciousness at grips with natural objects, not consciousness face to face with God in meditation, but consciousness of the consciousness of others—this is the primary focus of fiction. The novelist's assumptions, often unstated ones, about the ways one mind can interact with other minds determine the form his novel takes.

Point of view, for example, is a special case of the consciousness of the consciousness of others, perhaps the most important case, since it embraces the whole novel. The narrator, as much recent criticism has assumed, is a role the novelist plays, an invented personality who is often granted within the looking-glass world of the novel certain unique powers,

powers of ubiquity in space and time, powers of direct access to other minds. The basic mode of narration in Victorian fiction is neither dialogue nor internal monologue, but indirect discourse, that mode of language in which a man plays the role of a narrator who relives from within the thoughts and feelings of a character and registers these in his own language, or in a mixture of the character's language and his own language. Indirect discourse is therefore continuously and necessarily ironical, however mild or attenuated this irony may be. The juxtaposition in indirect discourse of two minds, that of the narrator and that of the character, is, one might say, irony writ large. An exploitation of the fact that one can in language imagine oneself as having direct access to another mind makes Victorian fiction possible. A Victorian novel is therefore a version of the dramatic monologue, a version in which the monologuist superimposes his own voice, judgment, and mind on those of the character. As a version of the dramatic monologue the novel may be seen as an extension of that commitment to the playing of roles through sympathetic identification which is an important factor in romanticism. There is an unbroken continuity from Keats's extension of his negative capability from urns and nightingales to people ("I am with Achilles shouting in the Trenches," he said in a letter.[1]), to Browning's elaborate exploration in his dramatic monologues of what Charles du Bos called his power of "the introspection of others,"[2]

3

to the structure of related minds in *Middlemarch* or *The Return of the Native* (1878). There are always at least two persons present in a monologue by Browning, the speaker and Browning himself, though critics have since the days of the first Browning Society been arguing about the way in which the poet is present in "Bishop Blougram's Apology" or "Mr. Sludge, 'the Medium.' " Often, as in the two monologues cited, there is a third person present too, a listener, so that a dramatic monologue by Browning is an embryo novel, as Henry James saw when he spoke of "The Novel in *The Ring and the Book*."[3] In the same way an epistolary novel might be defined as a series of dramatic monologues, each addressed by one character to another. The novel in letters is a simplified version of the form any novel takes.[4] In all these cases the writer plays the role of a narrator who can enter into the lives of other people and speak for the inner quality of those lives. Victorian fiction grows out of earlier forms of intersubjectivity in literature and is itself a form of intersubjectivity.

The narrator of a novel comes into existence in an act in which the novelist plays the role of a role-player. The character is a mask outside a mask. The characters in the novel, on the other hand, are unconscious of the narrator's knowledge of them. Nevertheless, they in their turn live their lives in terms of their relations to others. In most Victorian novels there is relatively little detached self-con-consciousness, the self-consciousness of a single per-

4

son becoming aware of himself in separation from other people. In Victorian novels, for the most part, the characters are aware of themselves in terms of their relations to others. The integrity of the self-hood of each person depends neither on reaching the deep buried self by a descent into the mind in solitary meditation, nor on a contemplation of rocks, trees, and daffodils, nor on confrontation of a deity who is the ultimate foundation of the self. In most Victorian novels the protagonist comes to know himself and to fulfill himself by way of other people. A characteristic personage in a Victorian novel could not say, "I think, therefore I am," but rather, if he could ever be imagined to express himself so abstractly, "I am related to others, therefore I am," or, "I know myself through my relations to others," or, "I am conscious of myself as conscious of others." Much of the language of most Victorian novels is used to express the narrator's awareness of the characters in their awareness of themselves in relation to other people. A Victorian novel may most inclusively be defined as a structure of inter-penetrating minds. Therefore, analysis of work by the major Victorian novelists depends on discriminating definition of the forms of interpersonal relations in any given novel or group of novels.

2

The mode of existence of a group of related minds is fundamentally temporal. This does not mean that one should not think of these relations as generating a space, the interior space created by the words of the novel. It is inevitable that the reader should think of the field brought into existence by tensions between minds as a space and that he should use terms like proximity and distance, exteriority and interpenetration, superimposition and juxtaposition, continuity and discontinuity, to express the way at any one moment in a novel the narrator is related to the characters and the characters to one another. Moreover, the landscape of a novel—houses, gardens, roads, hills, and rivers—constitutes an interior space polarized by the tensions between the characters and expressing those tensions.

Nevertheless, time is a more important dimension of fiction than space. A novel is a temporal rhythm made up of the movement of the minds of the narrator and his characters in their dance of approach and withdrawal, love and hate, convergence and divergence, merger and division. The structure of a novel is a musical design made up of the constantly changing interplay between mind and mind which constitutes the action. Any given passage in a novel is a moment in that perpetually ongoing movement and draws its meaning from its multiple temporal relations to what comes before and after, just as in music a given note or chord has meaning only in relation to what precedes and follows.

The time of a novel is polyrhythmic. This results because each of the characters has his own time, as does the narrator. Each stands in a different relation to the present of the action as it passes, and each has his own temporal structure of recollection and anticipation. In any given passage in a novel these various temporal rhythms overlap or interact like the waves within waves in a great breaker making for the shore. The dramatic action of a novel is the temporal pattern made of the sequence of interactions between minds, each with its own temporal flow, as they move toward some equilibrium or dispersal of their relationships.

Comprehension of all the novels by a single novelist may perhaps best be obtained not by a comparison of motifs, situations, or characters from novel to novel, but by a comparison of the melodies created in the various novels by the interweaving of the minds of the characters. Through juxtaposition of these melodies a temporal pattern fundamental to the novelist in question may be identified.

3

A passage in Thomas Hardy's *A Pair of Blue Eyes* (1872–1873), will show how temporal perspectives determine form and meaning in Victorian fiction. This text is a good example of the way a multiplicity of times is interwoven in the texture of a novel. Human beings have in daily life such an extraordinary ability to sustain several simultaneous rhythms of time that the temporal complexity of a given passage in a novel is easily taken for granted. It may be detected by an effort of analysis which stands back from the passage and interrogates it for its temporal structure. The present moment in our reading of a novel is never enclosed in itself, nor is it just expanded by a single structure of temporal "ecstasies" like that analyzed by Martin Heidegger in *Sein und Zeit*. Heidegger's description of a movement toward a future from which the past arises as a "has-been" and is made present may be the basis for all temporal structures in a novel,[5] but in a typical passage in fiction there may usually be distinguished a number of different times superimposed at various distances from one another with that atmosphere between them which Marcel Proust calls "the poetry of memory."[6]

The passage in *A Pair of Blue Eyes* comes at a dramatic moment for three of the protagonists. Elfride Swancourt has already caused the death of one lover and is now in the process of betraying a second lover, Stephen Smith, in order to confirm her hold on a third lover, Henry Knight, once Stephen's best friend. To keep Knight she must deny that she has ever known Stephen, deny that she ever promised to marry him, deny that she once nearly carried that promise out. The betrayal comes in the instant of a look, a look of secret recognition which passes between Elfride and Stephen as her new lover helps her mount her horse:

> Her old lover still looked on at the performance as he leant over the gate a dozen yards off. Once in the saddle, and having a firm grip of the reins, she turned her head as if by a resistless fascination, and for the

first time since that memorable parting on the moor outside St. Launce's after the passionate attempt at marriage with him, Elfride looked in the face of the young man she first had loved. He was the youth who had called her his inseparable wife many a time, and whom she had even addressed as her husband. Their eyes met. Measurement of life should be proportioned rather to the intensity of the experience than to its actual length. Their glance, but a moment chronologically, was a season in their history. To Elfride the intense agony of reproach in Stephen's eye was a nail piercing her heart with a deadliness no words can describe. With a spasmodic effort she withdrew her eyes, urged on the horse, and in the chaos of perturbed memories was oblivious of any presence beside her. The deed of deception was complete.[7]

Many different times are present in the experience of the reader of this passage. There is his own time of reading, the sequence of moments which passes as he reads the words and of which he has at least a partial awareness. To read a novel is in one sense to be carried out of the real world and transported into an imaginary world generated by the words, but the reader never loses altogether his awareness of the clock time which passes as he reads and of the situation in the real world which that passage of time determines. The reader also has a more or less explicit awareness of the time when the author wrote the words. He knows a man named Thomas Hardy sat one day at his desk and wrote down these words out of his head and on the paper before him. He is also likely to know something of the facts of Hardy's life and to have heard that *A Pair of*

Blue Eyes bears a relation to Hardy's courtship of his first wife, Emma Lavinia Gifford, and perhaps a relation also to his earlier love for Tryphena Sparks.[8] Hardy wrote *A Pair of Blue Eyes* not in a pure ascent into the realm of imagination, but by means of a transformation of an earlier time in his life which must have been more or less vividly present to him as he wrote. The writing of the novel was an attempt to come to terms with that past by moving toward a satisfactory change of it into a fiction.

The chief means of that transformation is the creation of the voice and viewpoint of the narrator. The storyteller has his own time, a time very different from the doubling of past in a present reaching toward its completed change into a fiction which is Hardy's experience as he writes down the words. The narrator, it needs hardly be said, is not the real Hardy. He is a voice Hardy invented to tell the story for him; or, to put this another way, the narrator is a personality created by the tempo, diction, and tone of the words Hardy chose to put down on paper. Hardy's narrator, in this passage in *A Pair of Blue Eyes,* as throughout his fiction, stands outside the events of the novel in the sense of existing at a time when they have all passed. He looks back on the action after it is over or down on it from a height which is outside of time altogether. He has ubiquity in time and space and knows everything there is to know within that all-embracing span. Moreover, from his point of view the events of the story are real events which he describes not as they were for Hardy (imaginary, fictive), but as if they had a substantial existence independent of the narrator's knowledge of them.

Although the narrator is to the world of the novel as we are to the real world around us in the sense of not doubting its reality, he has a superhuman power of memory and clairvoyance. He can put himself at will within the minds and feelings of any of the characters at any time in their lives. He tells any one moment of the story in terms of a full knowledge of all that happened prior to that moment and after it. The omniscient narrator is the most important constitutive convention for the form of Victorian fiction, the convention easiest to take for granted, and the convention which is the oddest of all, the one requiring the most analysis and explanation.

Time of the reader, time of the author, time of the narrator—already I have identified three superimposed temporal rhythms in the passage. In addition there are the times of the various characters present in the scene, a different one for each character. Hardy has the good novelist's ability to single out in imagination two or three people from the vast multitude of possible characters and to concentrate not on their isolated awareness of themselves (Hardy's characters rarely have such self-consciousness), but on their awareness of themselves as aware of one another. This awareness dwells in time, and each character's consciousness of the others has its tem-

11

poral dimensions. In this passage, for example, Elfride and Stephen are aware of the way she has a
few moments before, during their visit to the family
tomb of the Luxellians, refused to recognize him.
They are also conscious, as Hardy makes explicit,
of all the earlier episodes of their courtship, episodes
which have taken up most of the novel to this point.

One of the extraordinary things about fiction is
the small amount of notation which is necessary to
give the reader a knowledge of the temporal depths
in the characters' minds. Part of the reason for this
is the existence of a similar depth in the reader's
relation to the novel. The reader is at any point
aware not only of the words he is now reading, but
also of the words he has already read. He has a
more or less confused and indistinct, but nonetheless
effective, memory of all those other passages, and
this enters strongly into his response to any passage
he now reads. He has a confused anticipation of
future passages, even at a first reading, partly because of hints about the future dropped along the
way by the narrator, who knows, of course, all that
has not yet happened. What the reader remembers,
in *A Pair of Blue Eyes* as in most Victorian fiction,
is the narrator's earlier presentation of the characters' moments of awareness of other people, for this
is what occupies most of the novel. The reader
remembers the earlier experiences of the characters
and the characters are shown as having this memory
themselves, so that two kinds of memory, each with
its own proper structure and quality, are super-

imposed. In the passage from *A Pair of Blue Eyes* the reader does not have to be reminded by the narrator of the last time Elfride and Stephen met, nor does he need to have reconstituted for him a generalized memory of all their past relations, since most of the novel has been made up of language which has been creating a vicarious memory in the reader to match the living memories of the characters.

The central event of the passage from *A Pair of Blue Eyes* is a look, one of those looks so frequent in Hardy's fiction, in this case a look which identifies the present moment of the relation between Stephen and Elfride as the betrayal of their past allegiance and therefore as forming an instant more important than most instants, a "season in their history," a turning point in its development. In addition there is the consciousness of Knight watching this look without comprehending it or seeing the temporal depths which enter into it. The interaction between these three minds is a good example of the relationship between persons which is characteristic of Victorian fiction. Far from being cut off from other people and seeing them from the outside as objects, Hardy's characters, like those of other Victorian novelists, often have a perfect intuition of the other person's heart. The Victorian novelists assume that each person lives within a field generated by the presence of other people. This field gives a man access to the minds of others, though that access may for one reason or another be barred. In this passage Stephen's eye expresses to Elfride an intense agony of reproach. His body and its gestures incarnate his subjective state and make it visible to her, although Knight does not see the agony of reproach in Stephen's eye at all.

At the same time as the reader is presented with this incomplete overlapping of three consciousnesses, he is also presented the separate quality of Elfride's mind, the chaos of perturbed memories which fully occupies her attention as she rides away from Stephen and which makes her oblivious of Knight and the surrounding scene. In this passage at least five different temporal rhythms can be distinguished: the reader's time, the novelist's time, the narrator's time, the time of the intersubjective field created by the various degrees of understanding which the characters have of one another, and the private time of one of the characters. Taken together they make up the modulating chord of intersubjective relations poised momentarily in this particular text, but ultimately including the whole novel, its author, and its reader.

This passage, like any other text in *A Pair of Blue Eyes,* constitutes itself while it is read as a present around which the rest of the novel organizes itself in a unified temporal structure holding past and future in the open as integral aspects of the present. Time is the fundamental dimension of fictional form not because the novel represents the "stream of consciousness," the "flux of experience," or "life as a process." These terms, like so many phrases current in the criticism of fiction, are implicitly spatial; they assume that time is a linear sequence, so that life is a movement along a preexistent road or river, past and future lying spread out before and behind like beads on a string, all moments side by side and of the same nature, extending infinitely in either direction. In fact, however, time is a constituent dimension of fiction because, as the passage from *A Pair of Blue Eyes* suggests, novels excel in expressing the temporality of the present as a reaching toward a future which will contain a reassimilation of the past. The novel is by nature an open form. In various ways it represents human existence as standing outside itself, as reaching toward an as yet unpossessed totality which will complete it and draw the circle of life closed. This "standing outside itself," this "reaching toward," are basic characteristics of human temporality. Any conception of fiction as having the closed perfection of spatialized form will tend to falsify the ways in which a novel may represent the temporality of the present as generated from a movement toward a finite future which will repossess the past. In the passage from *A Pair of Blue Eyes* there are many different related temporal rhythms, but each may be seen as another version of this presence of a present which lives and moves in the yearnings of its incompletions. Elfride, for example, goes toward a future love affair with Knight which will be lived according to her perturbed memories of her past with Stephen. The intersubjective tensions in this passage, as in so many other texts in Victorian fiction, are established by a reaching out of each person toward another who will, he thinks, bring to perfection his as yet unfulfilled selfhood. This dissatisfaction is the motive energy of love for Hardy, for Trollope, for George Eliot, for Thackeray. It is one of the most important ways man can experience his temporality.

The narrator's time, the novelist's time, and the reader's time have the same structure as Elfride's. The narrator stands in that future which possesses in potentiality the completed past, but he moves back through that past trying to bring it up to the future as a present actualized in words. The novelist seeks to comprehend his own past existence by moving away from it into an imaginary future which his story continuously generates, in one version of the hermeneutical circle of interpretation. The reader in his attempt to understand the novel is caught in another form of the temporal circle of interpretation, reaching toward a perfected understanding of the whole which is never attained, but which is presupposed as already existing in any partial explication.[9] To approach a novel by way of the reader, the author, the narrator, the characters individually, or the characters in their relation to one another is to encounter in each case a new example of the structure of temporality which provides the generative energy of fictional form. The criticism of fiction depends on exact discrimination of the versions of this structure operative in any given novel, no less than on discrimination of patterns of intersubjectivity.

16

4

Thackeray's *The History of Henry Esmond, Esq.* (1852) offers an opportunity to explore further the implications of temporal form in Victorian fiction.[10] In this novel Thackeray uses one of the conventional modes of the Victorian novel as a means of self-exploration. In this case the convention is that of the autobiographical novel, with its roots in the confessional form going back through Rousseau and Montaigne to St. Augustine. The novel is a good demonstration of the fact that an autobiographical narration, like an impersonal one, exists as a structure of overlapping times, interpenetrating minds, and interweavings of imaginary and real. Thackeray's sophistication about the alternative possibilities of style and point of view leads him to manipulate strategically the fact that the narrator of an autobiographical novel is an assumed voice and personality. *Henry Esmond* has probably a better claim even than *Pendennis* (1848–1850), to be called the most personal of Thackeray's novels, the one in which he most completely projects his sense of his own life and destiny. In *Henry Esmond,* Thackeray attempts more or less deliberately to confront his own life by the indirect means of playing the role of an invented character. Nevertheless, it is also true that Thackeray remains conscious of the difference between himself and Esmond and keeps a distance and power of judging which is present explicitly in his statements about Esmond and im-

17

plicitly in the form the novel takes.

Thackeray was in Esmond embodying and dismissing a false attitude in himself rather than yielding to the temptation to justify himself or to live out in a fantasy of wish-fulfillment the life he thought he deserved. "The hero" of *Henry Esmond,* Thackeray wrote to his mother, "is as stately as Sir Charles Grandison . . . a handsome likeness of an ugly son of yours."[11] "As stately as Grandison"— surely this suggests Thackeray's perspective on Esmond's self-righteous pomposity, as does the phrase "handsome likeness" the way Esmond is too good to be true, certainly too good to be a true likeness of Thackeray himself. Elsewhere he called Esmond a "bore" (III [1946], 72), and he told Anthony Trollope that the fact no one reads *Esmond* ought not to be surprising: "After all, Esmond was a prig."[12] Thackeray never speaks directly within the novel for his own view of Esmond, since Esmond has all the talking to himself, or almost all. Thackeray's judgment is present, however, in the way Esmond unintentionally gives the reader information which makes it possible to understand him better than he understands himself. Thackeray's view is also present covertly in the way the preface by Esmond's daughter Rachel, the only part of the text not written by Esmond himself, invites the reader, in spite of its filial piety toward Henry Esmond, to remember that the body of the text is Esmond's subjective reconstruction of his life, not an objective account by an unbiased narrator.

The structure of overlapping times in *Henry Esmond* is something like that of *A Pair of Blue Eyes,* but there are added complexities, and time is more explicitly a part of the theme. In *Henry Esmond* Thackeray attempts to come to terms with his own life by playing the role of the old Henry Esmond, now happily married to the first Rachel, living in Virginia, and as his life draws to a close sitting safe in his armchair writing the story of his own life, turning back in memory to his youthful adventures and playing in his turn the role of the young Henry Esmond, speaking of his younger self throughout in the third person. The aging Esmond can see his young self from a safe distance as another man, as a "he." The basic mode of discourse in *Henry Esmond* is a doubling of minds which is the analogue in the autobiographical or confessional novel of the doubling in the more usual Victorian novel by which an omniscient narrator, standing at a time after the events of the story are over, re-creates by indirect discourse the inner experience of the protagonists. In *Henry Esmond* the reader is constantly given two interpenetrating minds, that of the young Henry oriented in infatuated desire toward the future and that of the old Henry, sagely disillusioned about all but himself, and oriented in musing reminiscence toward the past. The novel is generated out of the interaction of these two consciousnesses. Surrounding this double role-playing, or latent behind it as a ghostly presence, is Thackeray himself. As Gordon Ray has shown, Thackeray's relations to his mother and to Jane Brookfield are the generative source of the feelings and events of the story. In writing "the last eight chapters of the first book of *Esmond* and the first two chapters of the second," says Ray, Thackeray "again lived through the whole course of the Brookfield affair and made it a part of his novel."[13]

Reality and the imaginary are, however, related in yet another way in *Henry Esmond*. It is, after all, a historical novel and contains descriptions of actual events and people—England's wars in the late seventeenth and early eighteenth centuries, Addison, Steele, Swift, Marlborough, the Pretender, and so on. As in all historical fiction, the reader is constantly moving back and forth between his sense that the novel is a faithful mirroring of history and his recognition that a historical novel can never be history but is a fictional transposition of history into the realm of the imaginary. If the style, and in the first edition the typography, of *Henry Esmond* are meant to recall eighteenth-century diction, syntax, and bookmaking, nineteenth-century styles and attitudes continuously interpose, as for example in the way the novel expresses not so much a mid-eighteenth-century view of history as the nineteenth-century Whig view which Thackeray had encountered in the first two volumes of Macaulay's *History of England* (1848).

Three times and three attitudes are constantly superimposed in the language of the novel: 1852, the time of writing; the time of Esmond's old age, when he is supposed to be composing his memoirs; and the late seventeenth and early eighteenth centuries, when the events narrated are supposed to have taken place. There are places in the novel when this superimposition of times is even further complicated, as when the old Esmond remembers returning in middle life to Castlewood and recalling his childhood there. The text here is a memory within a memory. Moreover, it provides the occasion for the novel's most explicit clue to the placement of the narrator: "How well all things were remembered!" says Henry. ". . . We forget nothing. The memory sleeps, but wakens again; I often think how it shall be when, after the last sleep of death, the *réveilée* shall arouse us for ever, and the past in one flash of self-consciousness rush back, like the soul revivified."[14]

The novel is that *réveillée,* a flash of self-consciousness which resurrects, after its temporary sleep in the depths of memory, all Esmond's past in an instantaneous panoramic vision of the whole. The point of view of the novel is not just that of an old man "at the close of his life," who "sits and recalls in tranquillity the happy and busy scenes of it" (I. 7. 73). The narrator is a man so close to death, possessing so perfect a memory of his life and so clarified a judgment of it, that it is as if he had already moved outside of time. He is like a revivified soul looking back from the detachment of eternity on the outstretched span of his life. One evidence for this is the way Esmond talks of the last day or

21

the last hour of his life as if it had already happened. From the point of view of the place where he stands, the end of his life as much as its beginning has become part of the past: "To the very last hour of his life, Esmond remembered the lady as she then spoke and looked . . ." (I. 1. 6); "Esmond could repeat, to his last day, some of the doggerel lines in which his muse bewailed his pretty lass . . ." (I. 9. 92).[15]

Henry Esmond is punctuated by references to memory which call attention to the fact that everything in the novel is seen through a gentle haze of reminiscence, at once distant and close, vivid and softened by time, as in Esmond's remark that his vision of the angry Rachel, after he has brought home the smallpox, standing with "the taper lighting up her marble face, her scarlet lip quivering, and her shining golden hair" . . . "remained for ever fixed upon his memory" (I. 8.88). In another place he exclaims: "How those trivial incidents and words, the landscape and sunshine, and the group of people smiling and talking, remain fixed on the memory!" (I. 1. 9). The law of this remembering is given in those texts which affirm the total presence of the past in the eternal moment of the narrator's memory: "Her words as she spoke struck the chords of all his memory, and the whole of his boyhood and youth passed within him" (II. 1. 180). Or: ". . . such a past is always present to a man; such a passion once felt forms a part of his whole being, and cannot be separated from it . . . . Parting and forgetting! What faithful heart can do these? Our great thoughts, our great affections, the Truths of our life, never leave us. Surely, they cannot separate from our consciousness; shall follow it whithersoever that shall go; and are of their nature divine and immortal" (III. 6. 422–423).

Esmond, however, is here talking of his infatuation with Beatrix. He is talking about it from the perspective of a time long after that infatuation is over, a time when he no longer loves Beatrix and can view his foolish fascination with detached objectivity, as well as relive it with its first intensity. It is immortally part of him and yet no longer identical with him. This doubleness is the fundamental structuring principle of *Henry Esmond*. The old Esmond relives the young Esmond's worship first of Rachel and then of Beatrix from a point of view which sees their folly in the perspective of a godlike detachment from all passion. He relives them as forever passed. Here the implications of omniscient narration in Victorian fiction are given an explicitly theological definition. To remember everything and see everything clearly, as Esmond thinks he does, is to see everything from the perspective of those portals of death within which the aged Esmond stands. Esmond is like a god or like a risen soul, "divine and immortal," or at least he assumes that he is. He claims to be outside the uncertainties of time, no longer living as an incomplete self yearning toward a future union with the woman he loves, but in full possession of himself by way of a full possession of all the times of his life. He looks back on those times, so he thinks, with a perfect extratemporal perspective on them. He sees their truth with unclouded lucidity of vision.

In chapter four I shall attempt to show that Esmond unwittingly gives the reader the information necessary to put in question his claim to possess godlike knowledge of his own life and godlike superiority to other people. For Thackeray, as for George Eliot or for Thomas Hardy, no man or woman can be a god for another. The complexity of *Henry Esmond* lies in the fact that it presents this indirectly, through the autobiography of a man who discovers that no other person can be worthy of his worship but who fails to apply this discovery to himself. Esmond sets himself up in solemn fatuity as a god worthy of the worship of others. This theme is dramatized with admirable subtlety in the temporal structure of the novel. If no man or woman can be a god to another person, then no man can claim to have a panoramic vision of the whole temporal course of his life. In questioning Esmond's insight into the meaning of his own life, the novel also questions the convention of fiction which supposes that an individual narrator can see things like a transcendent god or like an epic bard who sings under the guidance of some heavenly muse. For Thackeray, as for the other major Victorian novelists, man remains within time and cannot escape from it by spatializing it. Omniscience is possible only to a narrator who is a collective mind rising from the living together of men and women in a community. In *Henry Esmond,* as in *A Pair of Blue Eyes* and in many other Victorian novels, temporal form and the exploration of interpersonal relations are so closely intertwined that one may be said to be the embodiment of the other. If this is so, the critic may be justified in speaking of time and intersubjectivity as the fundamental formative principles of Victorian fiction.

NOTES

1. *The Letters of John Keats: 1814–1821,* ed. Hyder Edward Rollins, I (Cambridge, Mass., 1958), 404. The context extends Keats's statement: "According to my state of mind I am with Achilles shouting in the Trenches or with Theocritus in the Vales of Sicily. Or I throw my whole being into Troilus . . . ."

2. *"Pauline* de Browning: Extraits d'un Cours inédit," *Études anglaises,* VII, 2 (April 1954), 164: "l'introspection d'autrui."

3. *Notes on Novelists* (New York, 1914), pp. 385–411.

4. For an excellent discussion of the implications of form in the epistolary novel, see Jean Rousset, "Une Forme littéraire: le roman par lettres," *Forme et signification: Essais sur les structures littéraires de Corneille à Claudel* (Paris, 1962), pp. 65–108.

5. See Martin Heidegger, *Sein und Zeit,* 10th edition (Tübingen, 1963), p. 326: "Die Gewesenheit entspringt der Zukunft, so zwar, dass die gewesene (besser gewesende) Zukunft die Gegenwart aus sich entlässt. Dies dergestalt als gewesend-gegenwärtigende Zukunft einheitliche Phänomen

nennen wir die *Zeitlichkeit.*" For a translation see Martin Heidegger, *Being and Time,* trans. John Macquarrie and Edward Robinson (London, 1962), p. 374: "The character of 'having been' arises from the future, and in such a way that the future which 'has been' (or better, which 'is in the process of having been') releases from itself the Present. This phenomenon has the unity of a future which makes present in the process of having been; we designate it as *'temporality.'* "

6. "En Mémoire des églises assassinées," *Pastiches et mélanges,* 33rd edition (Paris, 1937), p. 108: ". . . la résistante douceur de cette atmosphère interposée qui a l'étendue même de notre vie et qui est toute la poésie de la mémoire." For a discussion of the concept of polyrhythmic time see Gaston Bachelard, *La Dialectique de la durée* (Paris, 1936), especially chapters 6 through 8.

7. *A Pair of Blue Eyes, The Writings of Thomas Hardy in Prose and Verse,* Anniversary Edition, x (New York and London: Harper & Brothers, [1920]), Ch. 27, pp. 302–303.

8. See Carl J. Weber, *Hardy of Wessex: His Life and Literary Career* (New York, 1965), pp. 75–88, and for a somewhat exaggerated account of the place of Tryphena Sparks in Hardy's life, see Lois Deacon and Terry Coleman, *Providence and Mr. Hardy* (London, 1966).

9. See Martin Heidegger, p. 152: "Alle Auslegung, die Verständnis beistellen soll, muss schon das Auszulegende verstanden haben." ("Any interpretation which is to contribute understanding, must already have understood what is to be interpreted," trans. Macquarrie and Robinson, p. 194). For a discussion of this idea in Heidegger's theory of interpretation, see Paul de Man, "New criticism et nouvelle critique," *Preuves,* no. 188 (Octobre 1966), 34–35, and see also, for a discussion of the opposition between linear time and polyrhythmic or hermeneutical time, Paul de Man, "Georg Lukács' *Theory of the Novel,*" *Modern Language Notes,* LXXXI, 5 (December 1966), 533–534.

10. See Henri A. Talon, "Time and Memory in Thackeray's *Henry Esmond," The Review of English Studies,* N. S., XIII, 50 (May 1962), 147–156.

11. *The Letters and Private Papers of William Makepeace Thackeray,* ed. Gordon N. Ray, II (Cambridge, Mass., 1945), 815.

12. Anthony Trollope, *Thackeray* (New York: Harper & Brothers, n. d.), p. 121.

13. Gordon N. Ray, *Thackeray: The Age of Wisdom: 1847–1863* (New York: McGraw-Hill, 1958), p. 181. See pp. 180–188, and also Gordon N. Ray, *The Buried Life: A Study of the Relation between Thackeray's Fiction and His Personal History* (Cambridge, Mass., 1952), for full discussions of the connection between *Henry Esmond* and Thackeray's "longing passion unfulfilled" for Jane Brookfield.

14. *The History of Henry Esmond, Esq., The Works of William Makepeace Thackeray,* The Centenary Biographical Edition, X (London: Smith, Elder, 1911), Bk. III, Ch. 7, p. 435.

15. Henri Talon, in citing these texts, justly observes that Esmond talks of himself "as if he were already dead" (p. 150).

THE ONTOLOGICAL BASIS OF FORM

1

THE PRECEDING CHAPTER WAS BASED ON THREE assumptions. First: a novel is made of words and in that sense is unreal or imaginary. There are no physical objects, no real people in any novel. Second: the words of a novel embody a structure of related minds. Interpersonal relations are the fundamental theme of fiction. Third: a pattern of related minds exists as a temporal rhythm. Time is the basic dimension of fiction.

These are three ways to approach the same problem. Any attempt to account for the relation of form to meaning in Victorian fiction will constantly encounter three questions crucial to the interpretation of fiction: the question of realism, the question of intersubjectivity, and the question of time. To explore any one of these is to come by an indirect route upon the others. Approaching *Middlemarch, Our Mutual Friend,* or *The Way We Live Now* (1874–1875), by any one of these roads the reader encounters a structure which is not supported by anything outside itself. It is also a structure which is incomplete. The gathering of its elements is never drawn closed in a perfect circle maintaining a fixed spatial pattern which can be grasped in a single glance. A novel exists in movement and openness. It never reaches the poise of perfection, the ring drawn closed. A Victorian novel is, finally, a structure in which the elements (characters, scenes, images) are not detachable pieces, each with a given nature and meaning, each adding its part to the meaning of the whole. Every element draws its meaning from the others, so that the novel must be described as a self-generating and self-sustaining system, like the society it mirrors.

These characteristics of the form of many Victorian novels are related to the historical situation in which the novels were written. The development of Victorian fiction is a movement from the assumption that society and the self are founded on some superhuman power outside them, to a putting in question of this assumption, to the discovery that society now appears to be self-creating and self-supporting, resting on nothing outside itself.

This determining ontological transformation puts Victorian fiction historically beyond that situation I have elsewhere called "the disappearance of God."[1] A poet like Matthew Arnold still believes in the existence of God, but finds Him nowhere immanent in the self, in nature, or in society. God, so it seems to Arnold, must have withdrawn from the world and must be present somewhere beyond or beneath or above it. Such a man centers his whole life on the expectation of a return of the power which will once more constitute a foundation for the self and for society. This power would be the source, as Arnold says, of a "joy whose grounds are true."[2]

Most of the Victorian novelists have a different starting place. The situation which they confront with increasing clarity in their novels may most properly be defined not as the disappearance of God, but as the death of God, that shocking event announced most explicitly in paragraph 125 of Friedrich Nietzsche's *The Joyful Wisdom* (1882; 1886), and investigated in Martin Heidegger's commentaries on Nietzsche.[3] The death of God is confronted by the Victorians too, for example, in Hardy's poem, "God's Funeral,"[4] and is presupposed in one way or another by many of the major Victorian novelists.

What does it mean: "The death of God"? This phrase is not just an atheistical slogan or battle cry. It has a precise metaphysical meaning defining the experience of Western man at a certain moment in his history. The idea of the death of God enfolds in a single concept several related factors.

It involves first a sense of the vanishing of any extrahuman foundation for man, nature, or society. This experience is unlike Arnold's sense of the disappearance of God. It means loss of belief in God's transcendence as well as loss of the sense of his immanence. God is now seen not only as no longer present within the depths of man and nature, but as no longer present beyond them either.

The annihilation of God transforms everything

31

for man, changing not only his experience of the world but also his experience of himself. It is associated with a situation in which human subjectivity seems to become the foundation of all things, the only source of meaning and value in the world. Nothing now exists unless I think it. This means that man has become creator and measure of all things, even of God. God dies when man comes to look upon Him as an object of thought like any other and therefore as dependent on man's subjectivity for His existence. Nietzsche is describing this assimilation of all things by man when he says we have been able "to drink up the sea," "wipe away the whole horizon," and "loosen the earth from its sun."[5]

When God is annihilated, at the same time man annihilates himself and annihilates also the world around him. He annihilates them in the sense of hollowing them out, emptying them of any substantial presence. When the gods "came to nothing," as Wallace Stevens puts it, we "shared likewise this experience of annihilation."[6] Human subjectivity comes more and more to be experienced as a lack, as a devouring emptiness, as an unassuagable hunger for some lost plenitude of being. At the same time, the external world is also emptied, and man has, as Nietzsche says, the sense of "straying through an infinite nothingness," the sense of being "breathed on by empty space."[7]

This evacuation of man's nature and of external nature is associated with an additional transformation of man's sense of himself. To define man as a lack, as a hunger for fulfillment, is to define him as will, as a spontaneous energy of volition which reaches out in longing to substantiate itself by the assimilation of something outside itself. When God vanishes, man turns to interpersonal relations as the only remaining arena of the search for authentic selfhood. Only in his fellow men can he find any longer a presence in the world which might replace the lost divine presence.

Certainly there is little of Nietzsche's open confrontation of these ideas in the Victorian novelists, but as Victorian fiction develops there is an increasing focus on intersubjective relations to the exclusion of man's relation to physical nature or to any supernatural power, and there is an increasing tendency to define man in terms of the strength and quality of his volition. Interpersonal relations come more and more to be seen as a conflict of wills. The metaphysical implications of these factors only gradually become clear in the work of the Victorian novelists, clearest of all, of course, in Hardy and Conrad, but some version of them is present in the work of all the major Victorian novelists.

What has the "death of God" to do with the threefold structure of imagination and reality, related minds, and temporal rhythms which constitutes the form of a Victorian novel? The answer is that one is the basis of the other. The form taken by Victorian fiction implies a new notion of structure, and this new structure derives from the new metaphysical situation. Because there no longer seems to be any supernatural foundation for society or for the self Victorian novels are likely to take the form of an incomplete self-generating structure, a structure in which the temporal dimension is constitutive in a new way. Victorian fiction often presupposes a concept of society not as a web of commensurate elements supported by some creative principle outside itself, but as a pattern of incommensurate elements. These in their play of sameness and difference bring into existence a society which generates its own immanent basis for meaning. The change to this new kind of structure is analogous to the movement from older ideas of grammar and lexicology to structural linguistics and transformational grammar, the movement, that is, from the idea that a word has an intrinsic meaning which is added to that of other words to form sentences to the idea that a word has no meaning in itself. Meaning, according to the new linguistics, arises only from the play of differences between one sound and another as they are juxtaposed. In Victorian fiction there is a parallel movement from a view of society as a system in which each element has a center and foundation outside itself to a view of it as a system which founds itself, as a sentence generates its own meaning. In establishing its own meaning, the new kind of society reveals a principle of meaning which was latently there, but invisible before the society came into being.

The presence of this new view of society is especially apparent in the relation of imaginary and real in Victorian fiction. The traditional concept of realism assumes that a novel is a verbal representation mirroring the society it reflects. The novel and the reality it mirrors are seen as disparate realms, one copying the other in a different form. In fact, however, the mirror image may be a way of bringing into the open the imaginary quality of reality. A multiplication of narrators is especially liable to have this effect. When a novel presents a fiction within a fiction within a fiction, the reality at the beginning and ending of this series tends to be assimilated into it and to appear as itself a fiction. This might be called the Quaker Oats box effect. A real Quaker Oats box is fictionalized when it bears a picture of a Quaker Oats box which bears in turn another picture of a Quaker Oats box, and so on indefinitely, in an endless play of imagination and reality.[8] The imaginary copy tends to affirm the reality of what it copies and at the same time to undermine its substantiality. To watch a play within a play is to be transformed from spectator into actor and to suspect that all the world may be a stage and the men and women merely players. To read a narration within a narration makes all the world a novel and turns the reader into a fictional character. An image mirroring in words Victorian society brings into question its possession of a supernatural foundation, but when its nullity in the sense of having no extrahuman basis appears, its substantiality in the sense of being able to found and sustain itself is also revealed. The mirror image which at first seems to hollow out what it reflects, showing it as a baseless game, turns out to reveal a new kind of authenticity in what is mirrored. Just as the novel is a verbal structure which creates its own meaning in the play of its elements, so the reality of society is its existence as a linguistic or symbolic game which has the power to create and reveal its own foundation. The foundation exists only in the relation of elements within the game. Imagination and reality are identical. It is the same on both sides of the mirror.

2

Dickens' last completed novel, *Our Mutual Friend,* is an admirable text in which to see this play of imagination and reality in action. The narrator of this novel is critic of the community consciousness rather than being a spokesman for it. He is a reflecting mirror of Victorian society which undermines what it reflects by turning it into language. To move from the real Victorian society which Dickens was satirizing to the novel itself is to move into a looking-glass world of fictive language. This language constantly calls attention to the fact that it is language. Far from affirming the independent existence of what he describes, Dickens' narrator betrays in a number of ways the fact that fictional characters and their world are made only of words. This then reflects back on the real Victorian society and suggests that it too has a fragile existence like that of words. The basic structural principle of *Our Mutual Friend* is a doubling, like that of a play within a play, or of a picture within a picture, by which different levels of language or of narrative consciousness are placed one inside the other to generate an oscillation between imagination and reality. This interaction tends to blur the distinction between real and unreal, nonfictive and fictive. The various levels in their play of reflection—mind within mind within mind, or metaphor within metaphor, or narrator within narrator—come to appear equally real, equally imaginary. The reader is the first level in a sequence of echoing strata which emerges finally into Victorian England and absorbs it into the special quality of existence which the novel embodies on every plane of its language. The reader too is drawn into the game and comes to recognize that both sides of the mirror have the same reality, the same on the small scale of linguistic details and the same on the large scale of intersubjective relations.

An early passage describing the great looking-glass over the Veneering sideboard is the text in the novel which most explicitly objectifies the pattern of reflections in the novel:

> The great looking-glass above the sideboard reflects the table and the company. Reflects the new Veneering crest, in gold and eke in silver, frosted and also thawed, a camel of all work. . . . Reflects Veneering; forty, wavy-haired, dark, tending to corpulence, sly, mysterious, filmy—a kind of sufficiently well-looking

veiled-prophet, not prophesying. Reflects Mrs. Veneering; fair, aquiline-nosed and fingered, not so much
light hair as she might have, gorgeous in raiment and
jewels, enthusiastic, propitiatory, conscious that a
corner of her husband's veil is over herself. Reflects
Podsnap; prosperously feeding, two little light-coloured
wiry wings, one on either side of his else bald head,
looking as like his hair-brushes as his hair, dissolving
view of red beads on his forehead, large allowance of
crumpled shirt-collar up behind. Reflects Mrs. Podsnap; fine woman for Professor Owen, quantity of
bone, neck and nostrils like a rocking-horse, hard features, majestic head-dress in which Podsnap has hung
golden offerings. Reflects Twemlow; grey, dry, polite,
susceptible to east wind, First-Gentleman-in-Europe
collar and cravat, cheeks drawn in as if he had made
a great effort to retire into himself some years ago, and
had got so far and had never got any farther. . . . Reflects charming old Lady Tippins on Veneering's right;
with an immense obtuse drab oblong face, like a face
in a tablespoon, and a dyed Long Walk up the top of
her head, as a convenient public approach to the bunch
of false hair behind . . . . Reflects Eugene, friend of
Mortimer; buried alive in the back of his chair, behind
a shoulder—with a powder-epaulette on it—of the
mature young lady, and gloomily resorting to the
champagne chalice whenever proffered by the Analytical Chemist. Lastly, the looking-glass reflects Boots
and Brewer, and two other stuffed Buffers inter-
posed between the rest of the company and possible
accidents.[9]

This passage is seemingly inexhaustible in the
complexity of its implications. It contains in miniature not only the linguistic structures of the novel,
but also its narrative structures and its structures of

reality and unreality. The looking-glass above the sideboard is here a representation of the narrator's consciousness: detached, neutral, objective, reflecting what is there to be seen, but in this reflecting showing what is mirrored as an insubstantial facade, a dreamlike mirage. This is, however, what the Veneerings and their guests are in fact, as their name implies. The mirror image reveals a latent reality which might remain invisible without the distancing of the reflection. The narrator's consciousness, existing nowhere as an object within the primary reality of the novel, is here given an implicit substantiality by being identified with a physical object, the looking-glass, which does have a solid reality in the novel. To represent the narrator as a mirror is to suggest that there is only one mode of reality in the novel, the tangible physical reality to which both the mirror and what it reflects belong.

On the other hand, there are many aspects of the language of the passage which call the attention of the reader to the fact that it is made of language. Veneering, his guests, his table, and his mirror exist only in words and can be encountered nowhere else. If the passage may be read as assimilating imagination into reality and moving the narrator to the "real" side of the mirror by identifying him with the mirror itself, it may also be read as assimilating the reflected reality into the insubstantial realm of language on the other side of the mirror. The passage is like those optical illusions which may be seen as inside out or outside in depending on how they are looked at, and can come, as one stares at them, to move with bewildering rapidity back and forth while keeping the same manifest structure. The text from *Our Mutual Friend* may be read as imaginary or as real, but in either case keeps the same structure of opposing elements facing one another from different levels of existence and sustaining one another in their interaction of sameness and difference.

The use of the present tense in the passage tends to efface the narrator as an active presence seeing events through the veil of the past tense usual in fiction and the standard narrative tense elsewhere in *Our Mutual Friend*. The absence of active verbs in the second half of the syntactic pattern which is repeated throughout the passage has the same effect. The narrator is an objective spectator, a seeing eye or journalistic recorder, intervening as little as possible in his notation of what is taking place before him, registering it in language which tries to avoid imposing a subjective pattern of words on reality: "Reflects Veneering; forty, wavy-haired, dark, tending to corpulence, sly, mysterious, filmy . . . ."

On the other hand, this sentence and the others like it can also be seen as a covert demonstration of the novelist's godlike power to bring a fictional reality into existence out of nothing. Words liberated from their usual function as the names of independently existing objects, persons, actions, or qualities, recover their primordial power to create a reality of their own. Each adjective in the sentence about Veneering is like a magic formula bringing miraculously into existence in the reader the quality it names. As each is added to the last Veneering gradually manifests himself like an ectoplasmic vision at a séance, hovering in the space behind the mirror, a space which is both the imaginary space of the novel and the inner space of the reader's mind. The mirror mirrors nothing, but generates its own images out of that nothing: "Reflects Veneering; forty, wavy-haired, dark, tending to corpulence, sly, mysterious, filmy . . . ."

There is, however, another important element in the linguistic texture of the passage: metaphor. In the interplay of various levels within the metaphors another example of the structure of sameness and difference may be seen. This interplay reveals the fact that there is nowhere here pure reality, nowhere anything purely imaginary, but always elements which are simultaneously real and imaginary. The passage is full of metaphors, latent and overt: the description of Veneering as a veiled prophet, or of Podsnap's tufts of hair as wings and as hair-brushes, or of Mrs. Podsnap as a rocking-horse,[10] or of Lady Tippins as looking like a face reflected in a tablespoon and having a dyed Long Walk up the top of her head, or of Eugene as buried alive behind a powdered shoulder, or of the butler as an "Analytical Chemist," or of the guests as "stuffed Buffers." The same articulation may be identified in all of these metaphors. On the one hand they affirm the reality of what is described by establishing two linguistic levels. If the description of Veneering as

41

a prophet or of Mrs. Podsnap as a rocking-horse is clearly a fantasy of the narrator, since there is no prophet, no rocking-horse, no Long Walk, no Analytical Chemist in the first level of reality in the novel, the establishment of the distinction between the two levels tends to imply the objective reality of the first level. There has to be a Mrs. Podsnap on which the narrator may base his vision of her as a rocking-horse. This is another version of the Quaker Oats box effect. If the narrator sees Lady Tippins as like a face in a tablespoon, the metaphor is like a reflection within a reflection. The second reflection gives reality to the first and leads the reader to forget that he is already at one remove from reality.

Moreover, a number of the metaphors in this passage accomplish a shift in perspective like close-ups in a film. These invite the reader to see through the socialized surface of the scene to the gross physical reality underneath, as in the "dissolving view" of red beads on Podsnap's forehead, or in the proximity of the spectator to Lady Tippins' hair necessary to see it as a formal promenade, or in the similar grotesque magnification which turns a powdered shoulder into something which might bury Eugene alive. These metaphors, in their incongruous incompatibility with the usual view of the reality they describe, destroy that view and give the reader access to the dissimulated reality underneath.

At the same time, however, the metaphors work in exactly the opposite way. They swallow up the supposed objective reality in the linguistic reality on the other side of the mirror. One of the fundamental traits of Dickens' narrative language is the way his characters come to exist as metaphors. What begins as a simile describing vividly some quality of a person who exists outside the turn of language used for him gradually assimilates the character to itself until he lives chiefly as the metaphor which sums him up. When simile turns into metaphor the reader is moved from the real side of the mirror to the imaginary side. The metaphor is no longer an external description of a character who has an existence independent of it. The turn of phrase is the character's essence. So the butler who in one paragraph has been spoken of as going round the table "*like* a gloomy Analytical Chemist" becomes simply the "Analytical Chemist" in the passage I have cited, and is spoken of thereafter throughout the novel as "the Analytical." In the same way, Mrs. Podsnap is first "*like* a rocking-horse," but the simile becomes the metaphor which is her leitmotif throughout the novel.

When this transformation is complete, the reader recognizes that the distinction between levels of language, or between reality and language, cannot be sustained. If the character is so vulnerable to the assimilative power of language, this results from his never having been anything but language in the first place. The butler is first called the "retainer," which is a word, and this word is made the basis of another transferred word, the "Analytical." It is not

43

a matter of word and reality, but of word and word in a self-sustaining structure in which one word draws its meaning from its relation to other words. The reader has once more moved within the mirror and sees what he encounters there as the interplay of different levels of language rather than as the interplay of reality and its representations. The reader has to do with a novelist creating an entirely fictive world rather than with a spectator describing a real world. Either of these ways of seeing the novel has its authenticity, for both the imaginary and the real have the same structure and substance, the structure and substance of human existence itself.

3

The play of imagination and reality in a novel like *Our Mutual Friend* may be seen as an aspect of the interaction of various minds and times. The ontological basis of form in Victorian fiction may be approached by any of these routes. The author, for example, exists on this side of the mirror, as a real person, while the narrator, whose role the author plays in bringing the novel into existence, lives on the other side of the mirror and takes the unreal as real. A relation between two persons in a novel, to give another example, is parallel to the play of imagination and reality in fiction. The selfhood of one character comes into existence only in his relation to another person; and yet the other person is radically different from himself, and can never be transformed into his mirror image, never known completely or absorbed into himself in a merger of two into one. Only in a confrontation of the incomprehensible otherness of another person can I bring into the open my own hidden otherness, the profound depths which are the secret ground of my selfhood. My selfhood, though it comes into existence only in my relation to others, is something unique and intrinsic to myself. Reader, author, narrator, and the characters are caught up in this dance of confrontations, roleplayings, and clashes of will.

The patterns of intersubjectivity in earlier English fiction are usually based on the notion that each person has a self or a given nature created and sustained by God. The person relates this self to others, may lose it or fulfill it in his relations to others, but he has it initially in the way a word is assumed to have meaning in pre-structural linguistics. In the Victorian novel this concept of interpersonal relations is no longer maintained. Now each person comes into existence as a self only through his relations to others. If Victorian fiction focuses on inter-human relations as the arena of a search for self-fulfillment, this search is governed not only by the apparent absence of God but also by the effacement of any ontological foundation for the self. This lack motivates the longing for other people. The other in his difference from me or distance from me and in the difficulty I experience in joining myself to him completely is a means by which I can bring into the open my sense of alienation from my real self.

Just as I can never, as long as I live, possess my own death, but carry it within myself as the void which is a covert revelation of my being, so my desire for another person reveals the incompleteness which divides me from myself.

The temporal structure of a novel, whether it is looked at from the point of view of the reader seeking to achieve a total grasp of the novel, or from the point of view of the narrator telling his story, or from the point of view of the characters seeking to fill the hollow in their hearts and come to coincide fully with themselves, is also an expression of the way man is alienated from the ground of his being, that proximity of the distant which haunts him like a tune he cannot quite remember, or like something half-glimpsed out of the corner of his eye. Temporality, as Georg Lukács in *The Theory of the Novel* long ago saw,[11] is therefore constitutive for fiction in a way it can never be for the epic or for literature of the ages of belief in an independently existing eternal realm.

If this is true, one may identify a further damaging distortion introduced into the criticism of fiction by the concept of spatial form. A spatial structure is easiest to think of as an assemblage of elements, each with its separate meaning, all arranged in a fixed pattern to establish a total significance. This conception of form falsifies the actual mode of existence of a novel, the way in which it is a temporal structure constantly creating its own meaning. As E. K. Brown and others have suggested,[12] music provides a useful analogy for this aspect of fictional form. While a piece of music is going on the pattern of the whole in its incompleteness is held out in the open. A constantly changing rhythm of references and cross-references is sustained in living movement, each new moment of the music constituting itself as the center of the whole, or, rather, since the form is not yet finished, constituting itself as the failure of any moment to be the perfect center, the point around which the whole can organize itself in a complete circular pattern.

The concept of polyrhythmic time may be recalled here. Just as there are different levels of time in any moment of the music—any given chord, any moment of the dialogue between a solo instrument and the orchestra—so in a novel by Trollope or by George Eliot there is a tension between the individual time of the protagonist and the embracing time of the omnitemporal narrator. While the concerto or the novel continues the circle of form is kept open in a continually renewed, continually unsuccessful attempt of time to become space. The last moment in a novel, like the last note or chord in a piece of music, is privileged, but privileged not because the circle is now at last brought round and full. The last moment fails to do this any more than any of the other moments, fails, for example, in the still remaining incongruity between what the narrator knows and what the protagonist knows, or in the openness toward the future of the remaining characters after the death of the protagonist, or in the inability of the reader to hold all the parts of the novel in his mind at once, or in the sense the reader has that all the implications of the story have not after all been exhausted. There still remains, the reader feels, much more to say, so that the novel could be rewritten in a much longer form, and that longer version again lengthened, and so on indefinitely. The silence after the last word of a novel, like the silence after the last note of a piece of music, is by no means the silence of triumphantly perfected form.[13] It is rather a stillness in which the reader experiences a poignant sense of loss, the vanishing of the formative energy of the work. This secret source of form was never reached while the novel continued, but was held open as a possibility toward which each page separately reached, as each note in a musical composition reaches out toward the whole. When the novel is over the sense of that possibility is lost, and this generates a feeling of nostalgia, of regret for having lost the last glimpse of a marvelous country which can be seen afar not when the music or the novel is over, but only while it is still going on in its continuous failure to be perfect or perfectable.

NOTES

1. See *The Disappearance of God: Five Nineteenth-Century Writers* (Cambridge, Mass., 1963).
2. "Obermann Once More," 1. 238, *Poetical Works*, ed. C. B. Tinker and H. F. Lowry (London, 1950), p. 320.

3. See Friedrich Nietzsche, *Die fröhliche Wissenschaft, Werke,* ed. Karl Schlechta, II (München, 1954), pp. 126–128; Martin Heidegger, "Nietzsches Wort 'Gott ist tot,' " *Holzwege* (Frankfurt am Main, 1950); ibid., *Nietzsche,* 2 vols. (Pfullingen, 1961).

4. Thomas Hardy, *Collected Poems* (London: Macmillan, 1952), pp. 307–309.

5. *Werke,* p. 127: "das Meer auszutrinken"; "den ganzen Horizont wegzuwischen"; "diese Erde von ihrer Sonne losketteten."

6. *Opus Posthumous,* ed. S. F. Morse (New York, 1957), pp. 206–207.

7. *Werke,* p. 127: "Irren wir nicht wie durch ein unendliches Nichts? Haucht uns nicht der leere Raum an?"

8. S. L. Bethell, in *Shakespeare and the Popular Dramatic Tradition* (Durham, North Carolina, 1944), p. 39, uses a similar image to describe the effect of the play within a play in Elizabethan drama: "I remember a certain biscuit-tin which always gave me, as a small boy, a distinct sense of the 'numinous.' It had on it a picture of a boy holding a tin just like the real one, and on the tin the boy held was another picture of a boy holding a tin. . . . The 'play-within-the-play' . . . illustrates the same preoccupation. An audience watches a stage audience watching a play and so becomes simultaneously aware of three planes of reality."

9. Charles Dickens, *Our Mutual Friend,* The Nonesuch Dickens, ed. Arthur Waugh, Hugh Walpole, Walter Dexter, and Thomas Hatton (Bloomsbury: The Nonesuch Press, 1938), Bk. I, Ch. 2, pp. 12–13.

10. This is arrived at by way of the reference to Professor Owen (Sir Richard Owen [1804–1892]), a Victorian scientist who studied bone and fossil remains of animals.

11. See *Die Theorie des Romans* (Neuwied und Berlin, 1963), pp. 125–126: "Die Zeit kann erst dann konstitutiv werden, wenn die Verbundenheit mit der transzendentalen

Heimat aufgehört hat . . . . Nur im Roman, dessen Stoff das Suchen-müssen und das Nicht-finden-Können des Wesens ausmacht, ist die Zeit mit der Form mitgesetzt . . . . Im Roman trennen sich Sinn und Leben und damit das Wesenhafte und Zeitliche; man kann fast sagen: die ganze innere Handlung des Romans ist nichts als ein Kampf gegen die Macht der Zeit." ("Time can first became constitutive only when the connection with the transcendental homeland has broken. . . . Only in the novel, the content of which consists in a necessary search for essence and in an inability to find it, is time connected with the form . . . . In the novel, meaning and life separate and, with them, essence and temporality; one could almost say that the whole inner action of the novel is nothing but a struggle against the power of time.") *Die Theorie des Romans* was first published in 1914–1915. See, however, pp. 533–534 of the article by Paul de Man cited earlier (in footnote 9 of Chapter 1), for a critique of Lukács' concept of time in fiction.

12. See E. K. Brown, *Rhythm in the Novel* (Toronto, 1950).

13. As Ford Madox Ford argued when he said that in the last lines of a story a "lightning flash is thrown back over the whole story and all its parts fall into place" (*The March of Literature from Confucius' Day to Our Own* [New York, 1938], p. 579). See Frank Kermode, *The Sense of an Ending: Studies in the Theory of Fiction* (New York, 1967), for a brilliant discussion of different senses of time in literature. See also Alan Friedman, *The Turn of the Novel* (New York, 1966), for a provocative analysis of open form in twentieth-century English fiction. I differ from Friedman, however, in believing that the novel by nature tends to have an open form. Temporal form is open form. Twentieth-century English fiction, in my view, is not so much an innovation or "turn" in the tradition of the novel as a clearer revelation of implications previously latent in fictional form.

THE NARRATOR AS
GENERAL CONSCIOUSNESS

1

EACH VICTORIAN NOVEL IS UNIQUE AND CAN BE fully understood only on its own terms. It also participates in a period style and makes use in its own way of conventions peculiar to Victorian England. To put the works of Dickens, Thackeray, George Eliot, Trollope, Meredith, and Hardy side by side, moving back and forth from one to another, may make it possible to identify more exactly a form which recurs from novelist to novelist.

2

Each of these novelists begins in one way or another in isolation from the society which will be the subject of his fiction. Sometimes this derives from the class structure of English society, as George Meredith was acutely conscious of the fact that he was the son and grandson of tailors and had not inherited by birth the status of a gentleman. At first he saw as an outsider the aristocracy and upper middle class which were to be his chosen subject.

Sometimes, as in the case of Thackeray, the exclusion is somewhat attenuated, but no less fundamental as a generative force behind the fiction. Though Thackeray inherited a secure place in society, a degree of alienation may be identified in his lonely and unhappy childhood, when he was often a solitary child among adults. Moreover, he was a member of the group of Anglo-Indians, the families of English civil servants and officers who had lived in India, often for many years. These families sent their children back to England to be educated and returned themselves to form an upper middle class interpenetrating the larger one, but slightly apart from it and conscious of its difference. Thackeray's theme is the search for happiness in the context of a society which is seen from the outside with a certain amount of critical detachment, as something alien to the individual and as a dubious aid to his attempt to find something solid on which to base his life. From early in his writing career, for example in *The Book of Snobs* (1846), Thackeray believes that anyone who accepts without question his place in society as the measure of his worth is deceived and deceiving. Like Marcel Proust, he has an acute sensitivity to the pattern of snobbery whereby value is never recognized directly, but is always reflected from one person or group to another, so that a woman is desirable and a man has power only because they seem desirable or manly to others. In order to see this clearly Thackeray must to some degree be outside the society which is collectively bewitched by the magic formulas of snobbery.

George Eliot's habitual theme is the provincial

society she has known as a child. Her loss of faith in Christianity, her association with the group of radical London intellectuals centered around John Chapman and the *Westminster Review,* and above all her irregular liaison with George Henry Lewes cut her off from communication with her beloved Warwickshire. Just as James Joyce's one subject is the Dublin from which he has exiled himself, so George Eliot, from a similar isolation, turns back in nostalgic revery to memories of her childhood and begins writing the novels which re-create Warwickshire society and explore its laws.

The origins of Dickens' creativity may be seen in his childhood experience of alienation. His account of this turning point in his life is given in the autobiographical fragment included in Forster's *Life.* The fragment was written shortly before Dickens began writing *David Copperfield,* that most intimate of his novels, the one most obviously a fictional expression of his sense of his own life. The autobiographical fragment, like *David Copperfield,* is not an objective account of what Dickens' childhood experiences were like when he first experienced them. His childhood is seen through the mists of time and in terms of his intervening experiences. It is described in the language of the adult Dickens. As in *David Copperfield,* the reader is presented with two superimposed minds, the mind of the adult Dickens re-creating in words the mind of the child Dickens. Nevertheless, Dickens' description of his experiences in the blacking factory provides the best access we have to the moment when Dickens' sense of himself crystallized in its more or less permanent form:

> It is wonderful to me how I could have been so easily cast away at such an age. It is wonderful to me that, even after my descent into the poor little drudge I had been since we came to London, no one had compassion enough on me—a child of singular abilities, quick, eager, delicate, and soon hurt, bodily or mentally—to suggest that something might have been spared, as certainly it might have been, to place me at at any common school. Our friends, I take it, were tired out. No one made any sign. My father and mother were quite satisfied.[1]

Then follows the description of his menial work in the blacking factory:

> No words can express the secret agony of my soul as I sunk into this companionship; compared these every-day associates with those of my happier childhood; and felt my early hopes of growing up to be a learned and distinguished man, crushed in my breast. The deep remembrance of the sense I had of being utterly neglected and hopeless; of the shame I felt in my position; of the misery it was to my young heart to believe that, day by day, what I had learned, and thought, and delighted in, and raised my fancy and my emulation up by, was passing away from me, never to be brought back any more; cannot be written. My whole nature was so penetrated with the grief and humiliation of such considerations, that even now, famous and caressed and happy, I often forget in my dreams that I have a dear wife and children; even that I am a man; and wander desolately back to that time of my life. (p. 53)

Central in the young Dickens' suffering is his sense of being abandoned, cast away by his parents. He feels cut off from the community of family and friends within which he has earlier lived. This group has withdrawn into itself, leaving Dickens outside its charmed circle of security. It makes no effort to communicate with the boy they have made into an outsider: "No one made any sign." Replacing the happy intimacy of his childhood there is the alien community of blacking factory boys, a community which Dickens sees from the outside as something in which he refuses to participate. In his isolation he feels the substance of his being, the basis of his hopes for the future, passing away from him, never to be brought back any more. In place of the substantial self he has had is being put a new self which is neglected and hopeless. If no one makes any sign to him, his own power of language, the power which would allow him to achieve a secure place in the community, is slowly flowing away from him, never to return. His new desolate identity remains all his life with him as his deepest sense of himself, something he wanders back to in his dreams, even when he is famous and caressed and happy.

The novels of Anthony Trollope seem in most ways so unlike those of Dickens in theme and atmosphere that it is surprising to discover how similar his starting place is. If Dickens' months in the blacking factory determined his sense of his relation to the world, Trollope's equivalent experiences were those schoolboy sufferings at Winchester and Harrow he tells of so amusingly in the early pages of his *Autobiography* (1883). Trollope's father was an impoverished lawyer who determined that his sons should go to a public school and then to Oxford. Here is Trollope's description of the result:

> Boots, waistcoats, and pocket-handkerchiefs, which, with some slight superveillance, were at the command of other scholars, were closed luxuries to me. My schoolfellows of course knew that it was so, and I became a Pariah. . . . I suffered horribly! I could make no stand against it. I had no friend to whom I could pour out my sorrows. I was big, and awkward, and ugly, and, I have no doubt, skulked about in a most unattractive manner. Of course I was ill-dressed and dirty. But, ah! how well I remember all the agonies of my young heart; how I considered whether I should always be alone . . . . The indignities I endured are not to be described. As I look back it seems to me that all hands were turned against me,—those of masters as well as boys. I was allowed to join in no plays. Nor did I learn anything,—for I was taught nothing. . . . I was never able to overcome—or even to attempt to overcome—the absolute isolation of my school position. Of the cricket-ground or racket-court I was allowed to know nothing. And yet I longed for these things with an exceeding longing. I coveted popularity with a coveting which was almost mean. . . . Something of the disgrace of my schooldays has clung to me all through life. . . . [I]n truth I was wretched,— sometimes almost unto death, and have often cursed the hour in which I was born. There had clung to me a feeling that I had been looked upon always as an evil, an encumbrance, a useless thing,—as a creature of whom those connected with him had to be ashamed.[2]

Like Dickens, Trollope was excluded from a society which he could only watch in longing from the outside, but unlike Dickens, Trollope could choose only total solitude as an alternative to belonging to the good society, not the corrupting communion of inferior associates. Trollope's sense of exclusion, like Dickens', takes forms which are important in determining the themes of his writing. Trollope wanted most of all to be popular, to be accepted by others. He suffered especially from being excluded from the games of the other boys. A game like cricket, with shared rules allowing success or failure to be easily and publicly recognized, is much like Trollope's later conception of English society and also much like the daydream stories which the young Trollope carried on from day to day and from month to month, "binding [himself] down to certain laws, to certain proportions, and proprieties, and unities" (p. 36). These daydreams, as Trollope himself says, were the origin of his art as a novelist. The metaphor of social life as a game recurs in his work, as do literal games and sports, like the fox-hunting which he loved and described so well.

If the young Trollope was excluded from the games of the other boys, he was also excluded from their language, that sustaining medium of the community. He was unable to learn Latin and Greek, and he had no friend to whom he might talk. Excluded from the speech of the group, he was reduced to muteness himself, as on that occasion when he was unjustly accused of a schoolboy crime and could not even speak out in answer to the master's apology: "With all a stupid boy's slowness, I said nothing" (p. 5). Even now, he confesses, when he is greeted as a school-fellow by someone who was with him at Harrow or Winchester, he feels that he has "no right to talk of things from most of which [he] was kept in estrangement" (p. 14). To return to society will mean for him being able to share in a communal language.

Thomas Hardy's initial position is a little different, although it is still a variant of the situation in which the other novelists begin. Hardy as a young architect and later as a writer in London was in the position of the son of a workingman making his way among gentlemen and ladies. This isolation by reason of class inferiority is an important theme in his novels, as in the courtship of Elfride by Stephen Smith in *A Pair of Blue Eyes,* or in the experiences in Christminster of Jude Fawley in *Jude the Obscure* (1894–1895). Nevertheless, Hardy's detachment seems to have been as much caused by an instinctive withdrawal as the result of being excluded by others. A text in *The Early Life of Thomas Hardy: 1840–1891* (1928), probably written, like most of the *Life,* by Hardy himself, takes the reader closer than any other text to Hardy's point of departure:

> One event of this date or a little later [when Hardy was about six] stood out, he used to say, more distinctly than any [other]. He was lying on his back in the sun, thinking how useless he was, and covered his

face with his straw hat. The sun's rays streamed through the interstices of the straw, the lining having disappeared. Reflecting on his experiences of the world so far as he had got, he came to the conclusion that he did not wish to grow up. Other boys were always talking of when they would be men; he did not want at all to be a man, or to possess things, but to remain as he was, in the same spot, and to know no more people than he already knew (about half a dozen).[3]

Though certain "experiences of the world" have preceded this moment, Hardy's vivid memory of it as an adult and his use of a similar scene in the early pages of *Jude the Obscure* suggest that it was a decisive coming to consciousness for him. Two aspects of the scene may be identified. The physical gesture of pulling his hat over his eyes expresses a withdrawal from involvement which is, for Hardy, instinctive. For him, to be conscious is to be detached. Consciousness is a passive power of observation which cuts a man off from everything. This native detachment of the mind is here ratified by a deliberate act of will. Hardy decides that he does not wish to move out from his safe center of watchfulness and involve himself in the world. He does not want to know more people or to own things or to exert his will over others. He wants to stay in one place, safely enclosed, and overlooking like a spy what is going on in the world. From a safe position of enclosure he will watch quietly what he can see through the interstices of his hat. This way of being related to things is habitual for Hardy. It appears

61

everywhere as a formative principle in his work—
in the relation to the world of his narrators and
characters, in the cool detachment of the speakers
of his poems, and, most elaborately personified, in
the Choruses of Spirits in *The Dynasts* (1904,
1906, 1908). A stubborn disengagement from life
generates Hardy's art.

In six of the most important Victorian novelists,
some experience of detachment from the community, whether chosen or imposed, constitutes an
originating moment which determines the writer's
sense of himself and his stance in relation to the
world. To be an outsider looking in, however, is
not yet to be a novelist. What step transforms these
passive and mute watchers into novelists? What
personal need is satisfied by the act of covering sheet
after sheet of paper with words which bring into
existence a world incarnated nowhere but in the
marks on the page?

3

The transformation which makes a man a novelist is his decision to adopt the role of the narrator
who tells the story. To play the role of the narrator of *Middlemarch, The Small House at Allington* (1862–1864), *Little Dorrit* (1857–1858), or
The Return of the Native is to move in an instant
to the other side of the mirror and to enjoy all that
immersion in society which has been forbidden or

feared. The Victorian novelists were in one sense manipulating accepted conventions in order to produce objective works of art. In another sense they used these conventions as a strategy to solve problems of their own. The writing of fiction was an indirect way for them to reenter the social world from which they had been excluded or which they were afraid to enter directly. If they had been excluded from it in reality they could at least belong to it in imagination.

All six of these novelists make use of one form or another of that standard convention of Victorian fiction: the omniscient narrator. This convention is so crucial to nineteenth-century English fiction, so inclusive in its implications, that it may be called the determining principle of its form. The characteristic work of each of these novelists comes into existence when he chooses to play the role not of a first person narrator who is an actor in the drama, and not even the role of an anonymous storyteller who may be identified with an individual consciousness, but the role of a collective mind.

The term "omniscient narrator" has tended to obscure clear understanding of the narrating voice in Victorian fiction. The theological overtones of the word "omniscient" suggest that such a narrator is like a God, standing outside the time and space of the action, looking down on the characters with the detachment of a sovereign spectator who sees all, knows all, judges all, from a distance. The narrators of Victorian novels rarely have this sort of omniscience. This perfect knowledge is rather that of pervasive presence than that of transcendent vision. When Dickens, George Eliot, and Trollope move to the other side of the mirror and enter into the role of the personage who tells the story they do not take up a position outside the world of the novel, as a watchtower of vision down on it. They move within the community. They identify themselves with a human awareness which is everywhere at all times within the world of the novel. This awareness surrounds and permeates each individual human mind and therefore is able to know it perfectly from the inside, to live its life.

This immanent omniscience is both like and unlike the knowledge traditionally ascribed to God. It is an authentic perfection of knowledge. The omniscient narrator is able to remember perfectly all the past, to foresee the future course of events, and to penetrate with irresistible insight the most secret crevice in the heart of each man. He can know the person better than the person knows himself, as when Trollope's narrator in *Phineas Redux* (1874), says of his hero: "No doubt Madame Goesler was right in attributing the revulsion in his hopes to Mr. Bonteen and Mr. Bonteen's enmity; but Phineas Finn himself did not know that it was so,"[4] or as in the way George Eliot's narrator in *Middlemarch* analyzes for the reader with pitying clarity the self-deceptions of Dorothea, Fred Vincy, or Mr. Bulstrode.

Immanent rather than transcendent, thereby lacking one aspect of divine knowledge, the omniscient narrator also has knowledge of a world which he has not created. God's knowledge is of a world and of human souls which he himself has made. He knows them because he has created them and sustains them in being. He remains within and without his creation at once, without as its cause or ground, within as its substance, that which is more intimate to it than itself. The omniscient narrators of Victorian novels, on the other hand, have perfect knowledge of a world they have not made. There is relatively little of what has come to be called the "antinovel" in Victorian fiction. There are few places where the narrator explicitly confesses that the novel is a novel, though many aspects of the narrative language may implicitly recognize this. For the most part, the narrators of Victorian novels talk as if they were confronting directly or in historical retrospect a world independent of their knowledge of it, but a world over which they happen to have extraordinary powers. The novelist himself knows that the world is an invented one, that it exists only in the words he makes up and puts down on the page. The narrator whose role he plays exists as much on the other side of the mirror as any of the characters. He takes the story as authentic history. He is like an immanent God who has perfect knowledge not of his own creation, but of the creation of another God, an externally existing world which he has somehow been able to penetrate, flowing into it like a ubiquitous sea or like

65

a pervasive perfume which can pierce the most hidden recesses, entering freely everywhere.

A good place to see the difference between the novelist and the narrator is in the juxtaposition of those brief prefaces Hardy wrote for reprinted editions of his novels and the first sentences of the novels themselves. In the prefaces Hardy speaks in his own voice and confesses to the fictitious quality of the novel, as in the first sentence of the preface to *Far From the Madding Crowd* (1874): "In reprinting this story for a new edition I am reminded that it was in the chapters of 'Far From the Madding Crowd,' as they appeared month by month in a popular magazine, that I first ventured to adopt the word 'Wessex' from the pages of early English history, and give it a fictitious significance as the existing name of the district once included in that extinct kingdom."[5] To move from this kind of language to the first words of one of the novels is to move in an instant to the other side of the looking glass, to be placed within the mind of a narrator who confronts in memory a scene solidly real and placed firmly in a certain time and place in history. A good example is the first sentence of *The Mayor of Caster-bridge:* "One evening of late summer, before the nineteenth century had reached one-third of its span, a young man and woman, the latter carrying a child, were approaching the large village of Weydon-Priors, in Upper Wessex, on foot" (v. 1. 1).

This convention of omniscient knowledge of an independent world is justified by the fact that the

Victorian novelists, when they go over to the other side of the mirror, place themselves in imagination within the mind of the community, or at least within the mind of that part of the community which most interests them. This means for most of the Victorian novelists the mind of the middle and upper classes. This mind is assumed to be already there. It has been brought into existence by the living together of a group rather than imposed from the outside by divine Providence. It is embodied in the already existing language of the tribe. The Victorian novelists tend to assume that each man finds himself from his birth surrounded by a transindividual mind, identical with the words he learns. This mind surrounds him, embraces him, permeates him, from the first day of his life to the end. To write a novel is to identify oneself with this general consciousness, or rather to actualize a participation in it which already exists latently by virtue of a man's birth into the community. For this reason the writing of a novel is for Dickens, Trollope, or George Eliot a way of escaping from isolation. The reader of a Victorian novel in his turn is invited by the words of the narrator to enter into complicity with a collective mind which pre-exists the first words of the novel and will continue when they end, though without the novel it might remain invisible.

The novel makes this general consciousness visible by imitating it in another realm, that country of the imagination which exists on the other side of the mirror. A man living his life in society may be so surrounded and permeated by the mind of his group that he only rarely becomes aware of the degree to which it is the medium in which he lives. To represent that mind in the words of a fictitious narrator confronting a fictitious society is to escape from the real society and to obtain a detached perspective on it which allows it to be seen as it is. Victorian fiction thereby performs an essential service of demystification. The act of providing a mirror image of Victorian society liberates the reader from his unwitting imprisonment within its magic coercion, and it gives him an indirect view of society which allows him to see its hitherto hidden laws. The reader of a Victorian novel, like the author of it, must be on both sides of the mirror at once, seeing the fiction as a fiction, as a cunning model in words of the society it reflects, and enjoying at the same time a sovereign inwardness gained through perfect coincidence with the collective awareness of the community. To be both inside and outside in this way is to escape the pain of mute exclusion and it is to escape also the danger of blind imprisonment within the community. Though each novelist uses the omniscient narrator in his own way, a similar strategy of narration may be identified in each.

4

Thackeray's *Vanity Fair,* first published, serially, in 1847–1848, is one of the most masterly exploitations of the Victorian convention of the omniscient narrator. It may serve as an initial example here. *Vanity Fair* is in its use of the convention in some ways a transitional novel, looking back to *Tom Jones* (1749) as well as ahead to *The Last Chronicle of Barset, Middlemarch,* and *The Return of the Native.* Like Fielding's narrator, Thackeray's showmaster of the fair speaks in a highly individualized voice. He identifies himself as an "I" and tells of certain specific experiences he has had, or of scenes he was witnessed. Speaking as if he were a wise man of the world sitting in a comfortable chair in his club, he mediates between the reader and the events, directing the reader's judgment and moralizing for him on the vanity of life among "a set of people living without God."[6]

On the other hand, Thackeray's narrator boasts of his power to go everywhere and see everything. "The novelist," he says, ". . . knows everything."[7] Thackeray's narrator exploits this power to the utmost, as in the movement from the end of the ninth number to the beginning of the tenth number. The former ends with the famous sentence: "Darkness came down on the field and city: and Amelia was praying for George, who was lying on his face, dead, with a bullet through his heart" (p. 315). The first paragraph in the next number moves to Brighton where, the reader is told, old Miss Crawley was "very moderately moved by the great events that were going on" (p. 316). A full account of events in Miss Crawley's household follows. Like Trollope's narrators or George Eliot's, the narrator of *Vanity*

69

Fair has perfect insight into what goes on in the world of the novel. He can enter at will into the hearts of all his characters.

His overt allusions to this power, however, slide over into something different—the confession that this is after all just a novel, so it is not surprising that the author should be able to know and manipulate his own creatures. The most famous examples of this are the passages which ask the reader to think of the author as the puppet master and the characters as his puppets. The preface, "Before the Curtain," introduces the reader to "the famous little Becky Puppet," "uncommonly flexible in the joints," "the Amelia Doll," "carved and dressed with the greatest care by the artist," the "Dobbin Figure," and so on. The last sentence of the novel returns to this figure: "Come children, let us shut up the box and the puppets, for our play is played out" (pp. 6, 666). These antinovelistic elements recall similar acts of self-commentary by Fielding's narrators. They move the reader back on this side of the mirror, or "curtain," to follow Thackeray's metaphor of a puppet show. Such alternations between speaking of the story as true history and speaking of it as a concocted performance keep the reader on both sides of the curtain at once, which is where Thackeray wants him. The preface calls the reader's attention to the fact that Vanity Fair exists on both sides of the curtain. It is both the crowd of spectators and the mirror image of these in Thackeray's puppet show.

The implications of the metaphor of the puppet show are reinforced by the elements of parody in the style of *Vanity Fair*. Thackeray was unusually self-conscious, among mid-nineteenth-century English novelists, about the arbitrariness of style, technique, and point of view in fiction. If one of his early books is *The Book of Snobs,* another is *Punch's Prize Novelists* (1847), a hilarious series of parodies of the popular novelists of the day, Disraeli, Bulwer-Lytton, G. P. R. James, Mrs. Gore, William Harrison Ainsworth, and others. This penchant for parody carries over into his major fiction, sometimes as a mild flavor of irony which lets the reader know that the narrator is gently mocking a certain narrative style, sometimes more explicitly, as in Chapter Six of *Vanity Fair,* which in the first edition had burlesque versions of one episode of the story, first in the Newgate style and then in the Silver Fork or "genteel rose-water" style of Bulwer-Lytton, Lady Londonderry, Mrs. Trollope, Mrs. Gore, and Disraeli.[8] Thackeray sees that a narrative style creates the reality it describes. Alternative realities may be magically generated by telling the same story alternately in different styles. Thackeray's aim no doubt is to tell the truth about society and about himself as a member of that society, but he is aware of the difficulty of doing this. A narrative voice, he sees, is always to some degree an assumed voice. Any novel is to some degree an antinovel, not a direct picture of reality but a work of art which reaches toward reality by going away from it. A novel inev-

71

itably contains in its language some revelation that it is a fiction. As such it generates its own linguistic reality rather than bearing a one to one correspondence to some objective reality.

The narrator of *Vanity Fair* moves from one assumed voice to another. One quality of his voice, however, identifies him as a perfect example of a spokesman for the general consciousness of the community. This is his use of the editorial "we." The novel is punctuated by direct addresses to the reader in which he is encouraged to think of himself as one of a vast number of other readers who share similar experiences of life and similar judgments of it. We are asked to identify ourselves with one another and with the narrator who speaks for us until by a kind of magical sympathy we lose our identities, are drawn into the group, and taken all together come to form a ubiquitous chorus of judgment, the whole middle and upper class Victorian community surrounding the stories of Becky and Amelia, and judging them collectively or allowing the narrator to judge them in our names. Thackeray manipulates this rhetoric of assimilation admirably. Here is a characteristic passage of insinuating appeal to the reader:

> It is all vanity to be sure: but who will not own to liking a little of it? I should like to know what well-constituted mind, merely because it is transitory, dislikes roast-beef? That is a vanity; but may every man who reads this, have a wholesome portion of it through life, I beg: ay, though my readers were five hundred

thousand. Sit down, gentlemen, and fall to, with a good hearty appetite; the fat, the lean, the gravy, the horse-radish as you like it—don't spare it. Another glass of wine, Jones, my boy—a little bit of the Sunday side. Yes, let us eat our fill of the vain thing, and be thankful therefor. And let us make the best of Becky's aristocratic pleasures likewise—for these too, like all other mortal delights, were but transitory. (p. 485)

In another chapter, the charming description of "How to Live Well on Nothing A-Year," Thackeray makes explicit the way in which the narrator, though he speaks nominally as an "I," speaks actually for a whole society and gathers the individuals of that society together in fraternal unity through the irresistible appeal of his speech: "How does Jenkins balance his income? I say, as every friend of his must say, How is it that he has not been outlawed long since; and that he ever came back (as he did to the surprise of everybody) last year from Boulogne?" (p. 350). The sentence which follows gives an explanation of the nature of the speaker here which may be extended to the whole novel to identify the narrator of *Vanity Fair* not as Thackeray and not as an invented voice of Thackeray, but as the voice of the whole upper middle class and aristocratic society about which he writes: " 'I,' " says Thackeray, "is here introduced to personify the world in general—the Mrs. Grundy of each respected reader's private circle—every one of whom can point to some families of his acquaintance who live nobody knows how." Then the narrator goes on, having affirmed our unity in him, to speak for us all and for our collective experience of the world: "Many a glass of wine have we all of us drunk, I have very little doubt, hob-and-nobbing with the hospitable giver, and wondering how the deuce he paid for it" (p. 350).

This strategy of establishing the reader's participation in a community mind surrounding the individual minds of the characters in the story gives the strength of a universal judgment to the questions which come just before the shutting up of the box of puppets at the end: "Ah! *Vanitas Vanitatum!* Which of us is happy in this world? Which of us has his desire? or, having it, is satisfied?" (p. 666).

5

I have already suggested that Hardy's narrator is an extension of that wide, detached vision instinctive to him even as a child and most elaborately personified in the Choruses of Spirits in *The Dynasts*. These spirits, Hardy said, "are not supposed to be more than the best human intelligence of their time in a sort of quintessential form."[9] The narrator of *The Mayor of Casterbridge* or *The Return of the Native* also speaks for this collective intelligence of mankind. Such a narrator is a capacious cosmic memory which contains the lives of all men and women of the past and can resurrect them after their deaths, focus on any one of them, the life of Tess, or the life of Henchard, or the life of Jude, tracing the pattern it makes as it follows through the fabric of

74

history the thread fated for it by the Immanent Will.

A passage in Hardy's first published novel, *Desperate Remedies* (1871), shows how this image was present to his imagination from the beginning of his career as a writer. A man who is engaged in life, Hardy assumes, is blind to all but what lies immediately before his eyes. Only the man who is disengaged can see the whole. In this text, the antihero of *Desperate Remedies,* Aeneas Manston, caught up in a crucial moment of decision, obtains, as a reflex of his absorption, its reverse. It is one of those times, so important in Hardy's fiction, when the perspective of the character approaches, if only for a moment, the perspective of the narrator. For Hardy, life is an all-inclusive web which the wide vision of the narrator can see in its totality, though most men are limited to their own strands in the cloth:

> There exists, as it were, an outer chamber to the mind, in which, when a man is occupied centrally with the most momentous question of his life, casual and trifling thoughts are just allowed to wander softly for an interval, before being banished altogether. Thus, amid his concentration did Manston receive perceptions of the individuals about him in the lively thoroughfare of the Strand; tall men looking insignificant; little men looking great and profound; lost women of miserable repute looking as happy as the days are long; wives, happy by assumption, looking careworn and miserable. Each and all were alike in this one respect, that they followed a solitary trail like the inwoven threads which form a banner, and all were equally unconscious of the whole they collectively showed forth.[10]

6

Dickens' narrator too is a collective mind, but of a different sort. The way of becoming a novelist was for him an escape from solitude may be seen in the fact that in his earliest fiction, *Pickwick Papers* (1836–1837), and *Oliver Twist,* he identifies himself with a secure spokesman for the judgment of the good. This narrative consciousness is an extension of the journalistic "we" Dickens had employed in his earliest work, *Sketches by Boz* (1836–1837).

The narrator of *Oliver Twist,* for instance, is a man who lives long after the events of the story have occurred. He knows how the story came out. The pompous formality of his syntax and diction show him to be a secure member of genteel society, sharing with the readers he addresses accepted habits of judgment and speech. From the safe position of his enclosure within this invulnerable community he watches the sufferings of little Oliver, the evil actions of the thieves, and the antics of comic villains like Mr. Bumble. Since he is in no danger of finding himself in Oliver's position he can make arch jokes about the hero's experiences. These function partly as an ironic rhetorical device to generate by negation the outraged sympathy of the reader, but the disproportion between Oliver's inarticulate sufferings and the narrator's ornate style maintains firmly the narrator's detachment from the events and experiences he describes. "The fact is," says the narrator, to give one example of this from the opening pages of the novel, "that there was considerable difficulty in inducing Oliver to take upon himself the office of respiration,—a troublesome practice, but one which custom has rendered necessary to our easy existence . . . ."[11]

Oliver Twist, like many other novels, is the expression of a juxtaposition of two minds, the mind of the narrator and the mind of the protagonist. If the experience of little Oliver, abandoned to dens of thieves and prostitutes, and in danger of becoming like his companions, is a dramatic projection of Dickens' sense of his position as a child, this experience is in the novel not only presented from the inside, as in those passages where the reader relives from within Oliver's terror as the prisoner of Fagin, but also shown as it appears from the point of view of the safely detached narrator. The narrator's mind englobes Oliver's in an insulating medium which may be identified with the language of the educated middle class, secure in its values and in its sense of being justified by divine Providence. The temporal sequence of the novel is the gradual approach of the mind of the protagonist toward that of the narrator. This approach is complete at the end when Oliver's awareness of himself as a separate person disappears. He is adopted by Mr. Brownlow and absorbed into the collective consciousness of "a little society, whose condition approached as nearly to one of perfect happiness as can ever be known in this changing world" (p. 365).

The narrator of a late novel by Dickens like *Lit-*

77

tle Dorrit or *Our Mutual Friend* is no longer an uncritical spokesman for the values of the community. He is rather a coldly detached perspective on society, a mirroring consciousness like the great looking-glass over the Veneering sideboard. But the narrator of these late novels is continuous with the narrator of *Oliver Twist* in speaking for a collective awareness. The narrator of *Our Mutual Friend* is not, however, the "Voice of Society" which speaks as a false chorus throughout the novel and recalls the complacent voice of the narrator of *Oliver Twist*. He is the community mind become aware of itself, liberated from its worship of the false gods of money and rank, turned back from a distance to mirror itself, and so to recognize its true nature.

7

The implications of George Meredith's use of the omniscient narrator are made explicit in the theory of the comic spirit, most elaborately worked out in the *Essay on Comedy* (1887), and in the "Prelude" to *The Egoist* (1879–1880). The latter was written in part to demonstrate in a concrete example the validity of Meredith's theory of comedy.

The Comic Spirit is defined in the *Essay on Comedy* not as a superhuman being, but as an exhalation or reflection upward of society, the expression of a collective wisdom, the "common sense," in more ways than one, of civilized man. "If you believe," says Meredith, "that our civilization is founded in common-sense (and it is the first condition of sanity to believe it), you will, when contemplating men, discern a Spirit overhead; not more heavenly than the light flashed upward from glassy surfaces, but luminous and watchful; never shooting beyond them nor lagging in the rear; so closely attached to them that it may be taken for a slavish reflex, until its features are studied."[12]

In the "Prelude" to *The Egoist* the "comic spirit" is explicitly defined as "the spirit born of our united social intelligence."[13] The "Prelude" as a whole may be taken as a characteristically Meredithian hyperbole personifying for the reader the narrator of his novel. That narrator is the comic spirit, a social knowledge which has been gathering over the centuries in the "Book of Egoism." This is "a book full of the world's wisdom" (p. 1) which the writer must condense into manageable length in a work which absorbs and concentrates mankind's joint sagacity. "[T]he inward mirror," says Meredith, "the embracing and condensing spirit, is required to give us those interminable mile-post piles of matter (extending well-nigh to the very Pole) in essence, in chosen samples, digestibly" (p. 2). The comic spirit is the supraindividual awareness of the narrator which surrounds the characters of the novel, Willoughby, Clara, and the rest, reflecting them in its inward mirror and penetrating them with its pitiless perfection of insight. This social mind is given a final personification in the imps of the comic spirit who squat in a circle around Willoughby and

79

the others, waiting for them to betray the first signs of self-destructive egoism: "Imps have their freakish wickedness in them to kindle detective vision: malignly do they love to uncover ridiculousness in imposing figures. Wherever they catch sight of Egoism they pitch their camps, they circle and squat, and forthwith they trim their lanterns, confident of the ludicrous to come" (p. 5). The narrator of *The Egoist* speaks for these imps of the comic spirit and their detective vision.

8

George Eliot's development of a subtle version of the omniscient narrator as general consciousness may be followed from an early novel like *Adam Bede* (1859), to a later masterpiece like *Middlemarch*. *Adam Bede* is an excellent novel in which to study the Victorian version of that concept of realism in fiction which, as Georges Blin has shown in *Stendhal et les problèmes du roman,*[14] is fundamentally paradoxical and contradictory. For George Eliot, as for Stendhal and for many others, the narrator of a realistic novel is a mirror reflecting as accurately as possible the physical, historical, and social worlds. This image appears not only in the first sentences of the novel ("With a single drop of ink for a mirror, the Egyptian sorcerer undertakes to reveal to any chance comer far-reaching visions of the past. This is what I undertake to do for you, reader."[15]), but also in the famous Chapter 17, "In

Which the Story Pauses a Little," perhaps the most important text for the theory of Victorian realism. In that chapter George Eliot defines her aim as a novelist as "the faithful representing of common-place things" (p. 270). She wants "to give a faithful account of men and things as they have mirrored themselves in my mind." "The mirror," she continues, "is doubtless defective; the outlines will sometimes be disturbed, the reflection faint or confused; but I feel as much bound to tell you as precisely as I can what that reflection is, as if I were in the witness-box narrating my experience on oath" (pp. 265–266).

This text is already contradictory in the way it alternates between the idea of a photographic picture of reality and the recognition that a novel is a subjective representation, therefore necessarily distorted. Nor does George Eliot avoid alternating between speaking of the novel as if it were history and recognizing that it is a fiction. Though *Adam Bede* is based on historical fact and historical incident, it is after all made up by the novelist herself. The mirror mirrors itself, not an external world which corresponds point for point to the sequence of the narrative. George Eliot's recognition of this is made explicit in her discussion of alternative theories of art and in her defense of a realism which represents not historical individuals, but types of common life (pp. 266–271). On the other hand, the narrator of *Adam Bede* speaks as though the events described were history and as though he were

81

someone who had gathered facts as a historian of life in a real Broxton and Hayslope might have done. An interview with Adam Bede, for example, is cited as the source of certain information. "I gathered [this] from Adam Bede," says the narrator, "to whom I talked of these matters in his old age . . ." (p. 272). There are, however, passages, for example the preliminary description of the Hall Farm in Chapter 6, in which the narrator claims the right of omniscience and becomes a magical seeing eye able to bring history into the present and move through space with ghostly agility: "Yes, the house must be inhabited, and we will see by whom; for imagination is a licensed trespasser: it has no fear of dogs, but may climb over walls and peep in at windows with impunity. Put your face to one of the glass panes in the right-hand window: what do you see?" (p. 103). The reader of *Adam Bede,* like the reader of *Our Mutual Friend,* is moved constantly back and forth from one side of the mirror to the other.

The puzzles of realism in *Adam Bede* are resolved in *Middlemarch* by the frank recognition that a novel is the world turned inside out and taken into a subjective realm by something like that "inward mirror" of which Meredith speaks. The narrator's mind, for George Eliot, is an "ideally illuminated space" in which "the imagination . . . reveals subtle actions inaccessible by any sort of lens."[16] The narrator works, like the scientist Dr. Lydgate, by means of "that arduous invention which is the very eye of research, provisionally framing its object and correcting it to more and more exactness of relation" (I. 16. 249). The narrator is an all-embracing consciousness which surrounds the minds of the characters, knows them from the inside, but also sees them in terms of their relations to one another and in terms of the universal facts of human nature which they exemplify. The basic mode of narration in *Middlemarch* is a form of indirect discourse in which the narrator first relives for the reader one moment of a character's experience, then moves out to generalize about that character, and then goes to a still wider level of generalization, the universal experience of mankind. A report of Bulstrode's conversation with his wife after Raffles has returned, for example, is followed by a long analysis through indirect discourse of Bulstrode's permanent quality of mind, and this in turn leads to a characteristic universal statement: "There is no general doctrine which is not capable of eating out our morality if unchecked by the deep-seated habit of direct fellow-feeling with individual fellow-men" (III. 61. 133). A few pages later, as at other crucial places in *Middlemarch,* George Eliot presents covertly the aesthetic presuppositions of her novel in terms of an analysis of the scientific method of Dr. Lydgate. In Lydgate's view, "there must be a systole and diastole in all inquiry," and "a man's mind must be continually expanding and shrinking between the whole human horizon and the horizon of an object-glass" (III. 63. 163). Perfect description of George Eliot's method in *Middlemarch!* The narrator is constantly moving back and forth between concentration on "minutiae" (the idea recurs in the novel[17]) of individual minds and the wide embracing awareness of a narrator who coincides with the total mind of mankind.

Here may be recognized the great importance for George Eliot's fiction of her acceptance of the humanism of Ludwig Feuerbach. Her translation of Feuerbach's *The Essence of Christianity* was first published in 1854. For George Eliot, as for Feuerbach, God exists, but not as the creator of man and the universe. God has been created collectively by men in their living together. For Feuerbach, "man is the God of man,"[18] that is, the personified ideals of the community are the God of the individual member of that community. "God as the epitome of all realities or perfections is nothing other than a compendious summary devised for the benefit of the limited individual, an epitome of the generic human qualities distributed among men, in the self-realization of the species in the course of world history" (p. xvi). "Theology," says Feuerbach, "is anthropology, that is, in the object of religion which we call *Theos* in Greek and *Gott* in German, nothing but the essence of man is expressed" (p. xv). This conception of God is the source of George Eliot's "religion of humanity," and the narrator of *Middlemarch* is precisely that all-inclusive "consciousness of the species" which was Feuerbach's definition of Christ (p. 269). The narrator is a divine knowledge, sympathy, and power of judgment which has arisen from the encounters of individual men with their fellows. This clairvoyance surrounds each individual as a pervasive presence. The novelist identifies herself with it when she enters into the ideally illuminated inner space of language, and this identification generates the narrative structure of *Middlemarch*.

9

The narrator of Trollope's novels is perhaps the most perfect example in Victorian fiction of the omniscient narrator as a collective mind. The Trollopean narrator is within his world, embracing it in a close encircling like that implied in Nathaniel Hawthorne's admirable image of Trollope's novels as "solid, substantial, written on strength of beef and through the inspiration of ale, and just as real as if some giant had hewn a great lump out of the earth and put it under a glass case, with all its inhabitants going about their daily business, and not suspecting that they were made a show of."[19]

Trollope's narrator watches his people with an equable sympathy, a sympathy so perfect and so neutral in temperature that it insinuates itself into the reader's mind until the reader identifies himself with the narrator's consciousness and is no longer aware of it as something other than himself. The narrator becomes invisible in a union of reader and narrator.

Trollope's narrator is a collective and immanent consciousness in yet another way. He speaks far less as a single person than does the moralizing narrator of *Vanity Fair* or the sermonizing narrator of *Adam Bede*. When Trollope became a novelist, he took upon himself the role of spokesman for the general judgment of the community of English ladies and gentlemen. There are, however, strata, distinct levels of awareness, within that collective consciousness. These account for the persistent tone of irony in Trollope's narratives. Surrounding all, like the glass case and its atmosphere, there is the mind which knows all and judges correctly, sees everything clearly in all space and time, like an immanent god. Within this there is the community mind, sustained from moment to moment by the living together of English men and women in their society as they share habits of action and judgment. This middle and upper class society exists only as it is embodied in particular men and women, and yet it transcends any one man or woman and survives the death of any. The community mind is more or less confused. It has within it clouds of uncertainty and misjudgment, cannot see the future clearly, misinterprets people, as, in *The Last Chronicle of Barset,* many people in Barchester think that Crawley has stolen the missing check, or as all the world is fascinated by the charlatan Melmotte in *The Way We Live Now*. Trollope's narrator speaks for this collective consciousness too, most explicitly in those many passages in his novels which tell the reader what "the world" thought about the action or situation of one of the characters. In *Mr. Scarborough's Family* (1882–1883), for example, the news of Mountjoy Scarborough's illegitimacy travels rapidly through the community:

> It was not many days after that "the world" was first informed that Captain Scarborough was not his father's heir. "The world" received the information with a great deal of expressed surprise and inward satisfaction,—satisfaction that the money-lenders should be done out of their money; that a professed gambler like Captain Scarborough should suddenly become an illegitimate nobody; and, more interesting still, that a very wealthy and well-conditioned, if not actually respectable, squire, should have proved himself to be a most brazen-faced rascal. All of these were matters which gave extreme delight to the world at large.[20]

Within this community mind are the minds of the individual characters. The narrator speaks for these in the indirect discourse which makes up such a large part of Trollope's fiction. Individual minds in Trollope's world are never detached from the community, consciousness conscious of nothing but itself. They are bathed in the presence of other people, aware of themselves as they are aware of other people, seeking self-fulfillment in terms of their relations to other people. In many passages in Trollope's fiction these three layers of consciousness are present together, each with its own quality of opacity or clarity. The temporal structure of each novel moves toward a resolution in which the various layers come more or less to coincide, all opacity

87

removed in a triumphant: "They saw it all now," as, for example, everything is brought into the open at the end of *The Last Chronicle of Barset,* Crawley is cleared of suspicion, and his daughter Grace is free to marry Major Grantly.

10

Trollope, like the other five novelists, escapes from exclusion by playing the role of a narrator who coincides not with a god and not with any individual person, but with the general mind of the community. In all six of these novelists the omniscient narrator is more than a conventional device of fictional technique. Such a narrator is a generative presupposition determining form and meaning in Victorian fiction. From the narrator as an "I" who speaks for the "we" of his readers in *Vanity Fair,* to the narrator who is the looking glass over the Veneering sideboard in *Our Mutual Friend,* to the narrator as the man-made God of *Middlemarch,* to the narrator as comic spirit in Meredith, to the narrator as beef-eating, ale-drinking giant in Trollope, to the narrator as the cosmic memory of mankind in Hardy, the narrators of many of the most characteristic Victorian novels are one form or another of a collective mind.

NOTES

1. John Forster, *The Life of Charles Dickens,* I (Philadelphia, 1873), 51.

2. *An Autobiography,* The World's Classics edition (London: Oxford University Press, 1961), pp. 8, 10, 14, 51.

3. Florence Emily Hardy, *The Life of Thomas Hardy: 1840–1928* (London: Macmillan; New York: St. Martin's Press, 1965), pp. 15–16.

4. The World's Classics edition (London: Oxford University Press, 1964), Ch. 77, II, 401.

5. *Writings,* Anniversary Edition, II (New York and London: Harper & Brothers Publishers, [1920]), vii.

6. W. M. Thackeray, *Letters and Private Papers,* ed. G. N. Ray, II (Cambridge, Mass.: Harvard University Press, 1945), 309.

7. W. M. Thackeray, *Vanity Fair: A Novel Without a Hero,* ed. Geoffrey and Kathleen Tillotson, Riverside Edition (Boston: Houghton Mifflin Company, 1963), p. 351. This text follows that of the Cheap edition of 1853, which contains the author's latest revisions.

8. See the discussion of these parodies in the introduction by the Tillotsons, ibid., pp. xxiv–xxvi.

9. *Notes on "The Dynasts" in Four Letters to Edward Clodd* (Edinburgh, 1929), p. 8.

10. *Writings,* ed. cit., XIV, Ch. 16, p. 354.

11. Ed. Kathleen Tillotson, Clarendon Edition (Oxford, 1966), p. 1.

12. "Essay on the Idea of Comedy and of the Uses of the Comic Spirit," *Miscellaneous Prose, Works,* Memorial Edition, XXIII (London: Constable and Company Ltd., 1910), 46.

13. *Works,* ed. cit., XIII, 3.

14. (Paris, 1954), pp. 5–16.

15. *Adam Bede,* I, *Works,* Cabinet Edition (Edinburgh

and London: William Blackwood and Sons, [1877–1880]), Ch. 1, p. 3.

16. *Middlemarch,* I, *Works,* ed. cit., Ch. 16, p. 249.

17. See, for example, ibid., I, Ch. 6, p. 86: "play of minute causes"; Ch. 15, p. 226: "minutiae of mental make"; Ch. 16, p. 250: "those minute processes which prepare human misery and joy"; Ch. 18, p. 274: "the hampering threadlike pressure of small social conditions"; Ch. 20, p. 298: "endless minutiae"; Ch. 23, p. 353: "nice distinctions of rank"; II, Ch. 29, p. 11: "quivers thread-like in small currents of self-preoccupation"; Ch. 41, p. 210: "curious little links of effect"; III, Ch. 61, p. 130: "the fact was broken into little sequences"; Ch. 79, p. 384: "small solicitations of circumstance."

18. *The Essence of Christianity,* trans. George Eliot, Harper Torchbooks (New York, 1957), p. 159: "Homo homini Deus est."

19. Quoted from a letter of February 11, 1860, in Michael Sadleir, *Trollope: A Commentary* (New York, 1947), p. 240.

20. The World's Classics edition (London: Oxford University Press, 1946), Ch. 1, pp. 10–11.

SELF AND COMMUNITY

1

I HAVE TRACED THE MOVEMENT IN SIX VICTORIAN novelists from isolation to the entry into one form or another of a collective mind. That mind, as James Joyce says of a different kind of narrator, "flow[s] round and round the persons and the action like a vital sea."[1] It enters into those persons and lives their experiences from within.

The protagonist most often chosen for concentrated attention by the all-knowing narrators of Victorian fiction is someone who echoes the novelist's initial situation of detachment. It is as if the writer, having escaped from his solitude into participation in the community, were to turn back in imagination to the life of someone like himself. From the perspective of his safe position of identity with the community he follows that life through its course. Personages in Victorian novels, it is true, are never aware of themselves in isolation from other people, but the ones who hold the center of attention have not yet fulfilled themselves by way of their relations to others. They exist as potentiality, not as actuality, as a hollow or perturbation in the midst of the surrounding community. This situation of unsatisfied desire makes them relatively introspective. The narrator concentrates on their sense of themselves as incomplete and follows their attempts to bring themselves to completion.

The novelist can discover through his reliving of the experience of such characters not only the nature of selfhood, but also the nature of the community. The structure of society is invisible to those who live unquestioningly immersed in it, just as the foundations of selfhood are invisible to someone who can take his identity for granted. By focusing on the lives of people whose identities are in question, Victorian fiction also puts in question the community. The narrator's analysis of the temporary failure of the central characters to coincide with themselves makes visible the invisible by means of the visible. At the end of the novel the protagonists leave the community altogether or dissolve back into it. When this happens the secret foundation of the self and of society vanishes in the happy coincidence of individual identity and social role. Victorian fiction, like fiction in general, has a single pervasive theme: interpersonal relations. It does not investigate these by isolating two people from their fellows and concentrating on the dialogue between an I and a thou, but sees them in the context of the community. Investigation of one is therefore also an indirect investigation of the other.

Many different forms of this exist among the various novelists. There is, for example, the dramatization in *Oliver Twist* of the alienated consciousness

of the orphan in its relation to the alienated consciousness of the outcasts of London. The danger for
Oliver is that one will become the other. He must
keep his soul from contamination in order to find
the identity he deserves and be absorbed into the
society of the good. Or there is the repetition in
many analogous plots in *Our Mutual Friend* of a
movement of separation from society which puts
many of the characters in the same situation of
watchful detachment the narrator has been in from
the beginning. The question for such characters is
how they can get back inside society without com-
promising the authentic selves they have discovered
in isolation. In Thackeray's *Henry Esmond,* to cite
another example, the hero at first seeks to establish
a proper identity by way of a relation to a person
who seems to have the substance-granting power
of a God. George Eliot's characters too seek self-
fulfillment in an ideal relation to another person.
This relation, they think, will transfigure their lives
and give them a transcendent justification, as Hetty
Sorrel, in *Adam Bede,* seeks a dreamlike happiness
in her love for Arthur Donnithorne and as Dorothea
Brooke, in *Middlemarch,* imagines that her religious
yearnings can be satisfied by marriage to Casaubon.
Meredith's *The Egoist* is a sophisticated investigation
of the theme of self-fulfillment in a world where the
individual needs other people, but also needs to be
free to develop according to his own nature, and
Trollope's many novels are admirably subtle explo-
rations of the conditions of selfhood in a world

where the self rests on nothing outside itself and yet can fulfill itself only by way of relations to others. Hardy's novels, finally, focus on the theme of fascination, the ever-unsatisfied desire of each man or woman to find in another person a center and source of himself outside himself.

All these novelists concentrate on the theme of love, and all in one way or another see the relation of the self to the other as an attempt to satisfy religious longings in a world where relations to God are blocked. To put this another way, Victorian fiction may be said to have as its fundamental theme an exploration of the various ways in which a man may seek to make a god of another person in a world without God, or at any rate in a world where the traditional ways in which the self may be related to God no longer seem open. Often this search for a valid foundation for the self is dramatized in a woman rather than in a man, in Thackeray's Becky or Amelia in *Vanity Fair,* or, more obliquely, in the Rachel or Beatrix of *Henry Esmond;* in the Bella Wilfer of *Our Mutual Friend;* in Dorothea in *Middlemarch;* in Clara Middleton in *The Egoist;* in all those charming and yet strong-willed English girls whom Trollope, as Henry James said, made his special subject;[2] in Hardy's Bathsheba, Elfride, Eustacia, Tess, or Sue. I shall try to identify several variations of the theme of self-fulfillment in Thackeray's *Henry Esmond,* in Dickens' *Our Mutual Friend,* in George Eliot's *Middlemarch,* and in Trollope's *Ayala's Angel* (1881).

2

A clue to the form and meaning of *Henry Esmond* is given by the imitation *Spectator* paper which Esmond writes, has printed, and put on Beatrix's breakfast table when he is at the height of his infatuation for her (Bk. III, Ch. 3). The paper is a reproach to Beatrix. It recalls an episode in which she forgot the name of one of her admirers and even the place where she had first met him. In the *Spectator* paper the name of the lady is "Jocasta," and the paper is signed "Oedipus." Here is a striking indication of the recurrent pattern of Esmond's life! It suggests that Thackeray, without benefit of Freud, was fully aware of the kind of desire which motivates his hero.

Following Thackeray's lead, the reader recognizes, if he has not already done so, that the novel is a chain of overlapping patterns, each duplicating in variation the last and each reconstituting the universal family relationships: mother, mistress, sister; father, brother, son. These configurations shape and reshape themselves in the various episodes of the story, the primordial Oedipal situation reforming itself over and over with a different dynamic structure and with different persons, as perhaps it did in Thackeray's own life. The tangled series of generations in the Esmond family allows Thackeray again and again in the guise of the aged Esmond to experience feelings of admiration for the father, envy of him, secret hatred, desire to displace him, love for the mother, pain at being rejected by her, joy at being loved by her, guilt for displacing the father and for desiring the mother, rivalry against the brother and sister, love for the sister, and so on, in inexhaustible variation. Almost all the people Henry meets are cast in one or another of these roles by the force of his desire and hatred.

Thackeray has an extraordinary power to invent situations which will embody these feelings and allow him to express them vicariously. Good examples are the episode in which Henry brings small-pox to Castlewood (I, 8), and the episode in which Rachel visits Henry in prison to accuse him of causing her husband's death (II, 1). The pattern is first established in Henry's relations to Viscount Castlewood (his real father, though he does not know this), and to the grotesquely painted Lady Viscountess who remains a foster-mother to him throughout the novel. The Oedipal structure takes its most enduring form in Henry's relations to Rachel Castlewood, to her husband, her daughter, and her son. After Henry ceases to worship Rachel as a goddess, the forces of desire are constituted anew around Beatrix. Ultimately Henry ceases to love Beatrix, marries Rachel, inherits his place as the head of the family, and puts himself in the place of the father.

These swirling configurations are punctuated by references not only to Oedipus, but also to *Hamlet* and to the story of Jacob and Esau alluded to by Rachel's name. Henry, to give one example, hears from the Lady Viscountess that Rachel is about to marry Tom Tusher, the rector of the church at Castlewood (a post for which Henry had at one time been intended by Rachel). He rushes to Castlewood to prevent the match with feelings which the old Esmond describes in retrospect as like those of Hamlet toward his mother: "But Tom Tusher! Tom Tusher, the waiting-woman's son, raising up his little eyes to his mistress! . . . Rage and contempt filled Mr. Harry's heart at the very notion . . . . Tom Tusher to take the place of the noble Castlewood—faugh! 'twas as monstrous as King Hamlet's widow taking off her weeds for Claudius" (II. 5. 225–226). This episode is the occasion for the reconciliation between Rachel and Henry after their year of estrangement following the death of Castlewood at Lord Mohun's hands, a death for which Rachel has blamed Henry, just as Beatrix is to blame Henry later when her fiancé, Lord Hamilton, is killed by Mohun in a duel which duplicates the first. Mohun plays throughout the novel the role of the bad father, the father one is justified in hating. "[N]o voice so sweet," says Esmond of Rachel as he recalls their reunion, "as that of his beloved mistress, who had been sister, mother, goddess to him during his youth—goddess now no more, for he knew of her weaknesses; and by thought, by suffering, and that experience it brings, was older now than she; but more fondly cherished as woman perhaps than ever she had been adored as divinity" (II. 6. 230). The chapter ends with an embrace which mixes diverse familial feelings bewilderingly: "And as a brother

99

folds a sister to his heart; and as a mother cleaves to her son's breast—so for a few moments Esmond's beloved mistress came to him and blessed him" (p. 236).

The language of these passages explains the true nature of Esmond's desire and explains why after this episode Henry turns his longing toward Rachel's daughter, Beatrix. Esmond's love, like loving in general in the book, is described repeatedly in religious terms. "Who, in the course of his life," says the old Esmond of his long-dead infatuation for Beatrix, "hath not been so bewitched, and worshipped some idol or another?" (III. 6. 422). The old Esmond's lucid insight into the folly of love is complete. Love, he sees, is displaced religious desire, a search for a divine foundation for the self in another person. For Thackeray, as for Hardy, no human being can be a god for another, and of each such lover it can be said that he "hath set his life against a stake which may be not worth the winning" (III. 1. 345). It may be not worth the winning because the person I love has no divine value in herself: " 'tis I that have fixed the value of the thing I would have" (III. 2. 373), I or the others who are mediators of my love, as Tom Tusher's supposed success with Rachel sends Henry flying back to her, or as his love for Beatrix is shown to be determined by her inaccessibility and by the fact that she is desired by so many other men: "She had but to raise her finger, and he would come back from ever so far; she had but to say I have discarded such and such an adorer, and the poor infatuated wretch would be sure to come and *rôder* about her mother's house, willing to be put on the ranks of suitors, though he knew he might be cast off the next week. If he were like Ulysses in his folly, at least she was in so far like Penelope that she had a crowd of suitors, and undid day after day and night after night the handiwork of fascination and the web of coquetry with which she was wont to allure and entertain them" (III. 3. 386).

The story of Esmond's growing up is the story of his discovery that no woman, neither Rachel nor Beatrix, is godlike or worth his worship. When he recognizes this he sets himself up as the divine father, marries Rachel at last, and allows himself to be worshipped by her: "Let me kneel—" cries Rachel, "let me kneel, and—and—worship you" (III. 2. 366). This transformation of Henry's attitude toward other people coincides with his change from a Jacobin to a Whig. Just as he abandons his search for a goddess who will make him happy and give him a substantial self, so he abandons his belief in the Divine Right which sanctions the Pretender's claim to the throne. In place of his worship of Rachel or Beatrix he puts a sober recognition that the lover consecrates the beloved and gives her whatever divine radiance she seems to have. In place of his belief in Divine Right he puts his new conviction that Parliament and people have the power to choose and consecrate their sovereign. The two themes are intertwined in the dramatic action when

101

James loses his chance at the throne through his dalliance with Beatrix, and Henry abandons his faith in both Beatrix and the Pretender at once.

If the clue given by the *Spectator* paper is followed through all its echoes in the novel, it reveals the fact that *Henry Esmond* is the story of Henry's failure to read rightly the riddles posed by the sphinx. The *Spectator* story has to do with a *lapsus,* in which Beatrix (here called Jocasta and therefore secretly also Rachel, mother as well as mistress and adored lady), has forgotten her lover's name. It is rather Esmond himself who has lost his name. Like the Oedipus whose name he puts to the *Spectator* paper, he has lost his identity and unwittingly seeks it through his relations to other people. *Mutato nomine de te Fabula narratur*—the epigraph from Horace[3] which Esmond puts at the beginning of his *Spectator* parody applies also to himself and to his failure to recognize that he is, like Oedipus, a man who will cause the death of his father and replace the father in his mother's bed. Esmond is an Oedipus manqué, an Oedipus who never recognizes his guilt. He is a prig, as Thackeray called him, above all in the sense that his narrative is an obstinately blind self-justification. He sees himself as an admirable man who has acted honorably all through his life, has been wrong only in worshipping Rachel and Beatrix, and has every right to slide into the place of the father, the king, the god, sovereign judge of all the others. "He is not like a king," says Rachel of the Pretender; "somehow, Harry, I fancy you are like a king" (III. 9. 455). Rather than seeking substance for himself by possessing the goddess Rachel or the "divine Beatrix" (III. 4. 398), he thinks he discovers that he has himself had this substance all along. He finds that he is the real heir to the Castlewood fortune and title, and condescends in lordly fashion to marry Rachel because she worships him. The preface by his daughter shows him being treated as a god on earth by all his descendants and servants in Virginia. The writing of his memoirs has given him the full opportunity to identify his guilt —to recognize that he has usurped the places of those who have stood as father or brother to him and to confront his indirect responsibility for the deaths of Lord Castlewood and Lord Hamilton, his secret identity with Mohun (whose name is also Harry), his inability to love authentically, and his proud self-righteousness. He has, however, failed to read the signs aright. Having sought a goddess who will give him a proper selfhood if he possesses her, he is disillusioned about other people, but not disillusioned about himself. He decides that he must be his own god, that he can give others the substance he has sought to get from them, and that he is justified in ruling over them.

The novel, however, has given the reader the evidence necessary to see where Esmond is wrong. The reader includes Esmond too in the description of the emptiness of human existence which Henry expresses: "So night and day pass away, and to-morrow comes, and our place knows us not" (III. 6. 428). Thackeray's pervasive recognition of the vanity of human life in a society without God is approached covertly in this novel. The repetition of the pattern of Oedipal relationships detaches this pattern to the mind of the reader in a stylization like the various forms of duplication or mirroring in other Victorian novels. This emergence of a recurrent pattern, achieved through Thackeray's expert manipulation of the temporal depth of the narration and through the doubling of mind within mind characteristic of the autobiographical novel, leads the reader to understand Esmond better than Esmond ever understands himself. The reader recognizes that, for Thackeray, no man can ever fill the void in himself, neither through his own efforts at self-justification, nor through his relations to other people.

In the incompatibility between Esmond's interpretation of his own life and the interpretation presented obliquely to the reader, *Henry Esmond* is poised between Thackeray's nostalgia for a time when the self and the community had an extra-human foundation and his confrontation of a new situation in which people must generate their own identities over the void within them by way of the interplay between one person and another in society. The remaining novelists I shall discuss are, each in his own way, further examples of this self-generation of the person by way of his relation to others.

3

I have argued in Chapter 2 that a complex inter-action of imaginary and real, in which each sustains and negates the other, characterizes the linguistic texture of *Our Mutual Friend*. A similar structure of self-creation is present in its play of interpersonal relations.

The comedy of *Our Mutual Friend* derives from the exuberance of its language. This may be seen in the introduction, one by one, of the various persons who constitute the large cast of characters. Each lives enclosed in his own milieu, but each interacts with the others in unpredictable ways. The charac-ters and their surroundings exist exclusively as lan-guage, as is the case in any novel, but here the fact is kept constantly before the reader. By way of a continuously inventive language Dickens creates the roles of Boffin, Wegg, Twemlow, Venus, and the rest, playing each of these roles by means of the words which bring them into existence. With each personality goes a body and an appearance, charac-teristic gestures, characteristic habits of speech (like Wegg's habit of misquoting snatches of poetry), and a surrounding scene which is like an extension of the personage, as in the admirable descriptions of Bof-fin's Bower and Venus' shop.

Another consciousness is always present, how-ever, that of the narrator. The narrator's mind con-stitutes the neutral mirror-space within which the characters and their milieux exist. Dickens plays the role of a detached spectator watching himself play by means of language the role of Noddy Boffin, Silas Wegg, or Rumty Wilfer. The narrator is present, for example, in the irony of details of language which reveal the blind enclosure of each character within his own language and within his own vision, as when the narrator follows Boffin's remark that he wants "some fine bold reading, some splendid book in a gorging Lord-Mayor's-Show of wollumes" with the cool parenthetical comment: "probably meaning gorgeous, but misled by association of ideas" (1. 5. 55). The interpenetration of two minds in indirect discourse which is the basic narrative mode of Victorian fiction is present throughout *Our Mutual Friend* in the enclosure of the behavior of the characters in the mirroring vision of the narrator.

This juxtaposition of two minds keeps continuously before the reader one fundamental theme of the novel. To the clear vision of the narrator the characters from all levels of society, from Wegg and Venus to the Lammles, Podsnaps, and Veneerings, are seen to be so blindly immersed in their situations, so limited to their narrow linguistic matrices, so bewitched by the false standards of their society, that they are alienated from any authentic life. The metaphors of the narrator act as a transformation of the narrative from one level of reality to another which shows the reader the dreamlike unreality of Victorian society. An example is the extended description of a Podsnap soirée as a bathing party.

The metaphor which makes reality into surreality and so provides a revealing perspective on society is present only in the narrator's mind: "Bald bathers folded their arms and talked to Mr. Podsnap on the hearth-rug; sleek-whiskered bathers, with hats in their hands, lunged at Mrs. Podsnap and retreated; prowling bathers went about looking into ornamental boxes and bowls as if they had suspicions of larceny on the part of the Podsnaps, and expected to find something they had lost at the bottom; bathers of the gentler sex sat silently comparing ivory shoulders." (I. 11. 152).

The characters, on the other hand, use language which is heavily metaphorical too, but they do this unwittingly. Each is trapped in his own language and takes its insubstantial substitutions of one name for another as solidly founded. Each lives in a dream world in which language is detached from reality—as in the splendid linguistic nonsense of the conversations of Wegg and Venus, or of Mrs. Wilfer, Lavinia, and George Sampson, or as in the unreality of the conversation of the "Voices of Society." The unsubstantiated language of the characters is one symptom of the falsehood of Victorian society. This society, in Dickens' view, is based on no authentic superhuman values, but is generated by the mutual establishment of credit. The public opinion of the worth of an individual is created out of nothing by mediated exchanges. An example is the self-generating propaganda which gets Veneering into Parliament. The pervasive symbol of this

107

theme, however, is money, the worthless paper manipulated by the "Fathers of the Scrip-Church" (III. 17. 699). Money is taken as an absolute value and the measure of all other value, whereas in fact it draws its value only from the collective hallucination of the community which agrees to accept it as valuable.

The novel seems to present only two alternatives: a man may be a worshipper of false gods, or he may be liberated into a watching detachment, as are the narrator and the reader by the revelations made through the narrative language. A man may be either in the world, bewitched by it, or out of it, a passive spectator of the scene. The dramatic action of *Our Mutual Friend,* however, shows on several plot lines and in several variations that there is a third possibility, a way of life which is both within society and outside it. The central stories repeat again and again a process of withdrawal and disguise. The character becomes like the narrator, a separated mirror able to see society from the outside and therefore able to recognize that it is a masquerade of false appearances. John Harmon after his near drowning and the false report of his death is able to enter life incognito and see Bella, the Wilfers, the Boffins, and the rest from a point of view like that of death. Mr. Boffin pretends to be a miser and sees those around him from the detachment this disguise provides. Eugene Wrayburn is freed from his sterile role in society when he is nearly murdered by Bradley Headstone. His plunge into the

Thames, like that of John Harmon, and unlike those parody baptisms of Rogue Riderhood, Bradley Headstone, and Silas Wegg, allows him to escape from the enslavement to false social values which has kept him from marrying Lizzie Hexam. Bella, just before the revelation of the identity of her husband, lives her life in a dream in which nothing is what it seems. Her experience releases her from her infatuation with "money, money, money, and what money can make of life" (III. 4. 521). To be liberated in this way from a hypnotized submission to the false values of society is to be able to confront the elemental physical reality which society hides, the reality of death, and the reality of human passion.

In Bradley Headstone such passion is stirred up, like a "raging sea" (II. 15. 447), by his love for Lizzie, and he becomes murderously destructive and self-destructive. His story is evidence that for Dickens at this stage in his life it is impossible to live one's life directly in terms of the elemental realities of death, physical nature, and human feeling. Each man must return from an encounter with these to reengage himself in society. This new involvement will be made from the perspective of a prior disengagement which sees society as it is. This means reentering society by improvising one's role in it as a game. Society cannot be anything but a system of conventional rules, exchanges, and substitutions which are like metaphors. As long as a man takes the metaphor as reality he is deluded. When he sees through the metaphor and takes responsibility for living according to it, he is still caught in a play, but now he sees the game as a game.

This theme of a liberating improvisation of roles recurs in various ways in *Our Mutual Friend,* for example, in the way Jenny Wren pretends to be the mother of her drunken father or casts Riah in the role of the fairy godmother, enacting throughout the story various nursery rhymes and fairy tales, or in the way Eugene marries Lizzie in defiance of the roles society would have them play, creating in their marriage something modelled on socially approved unions and yet existing in detachment from the given structure of society. The most important version of this, however, is Bella Wilfer's charming habit of improvising plays in which she and her father can escape from their unhappy home life into a self-sustaining dream. This allows them to express their love for one another in freedom from the obstacles of their unhappy family life.[4] If Jenny Wren is the mother of her father, Bella's father seems to her "not like a Pa, but more like a sort of a younger brother with a dear venerable chubbiness on him" (II. 8. 360). When Bella marries John Harmon, her husband and eventually her baby, the "Inexhaustible," are included in this game. Bella, John, the Inexhaustible, and Pa create in their joint play the authentic meaning of the selfhood of each. This meaning is not founded on anything which supports it or guarantees its validity. In this it is like the insubstantial game of "Society" which the Veneerings, Podsnaps, and Lammles play, the difference being that Bella and John have gone through an intermediate period of detachment. They know that the game is a game and that it is played over the realities of human feeling, the "true golden gold" of Bella's heart (IV. 13. 872), and over death, and over elemental matter, dangerous and alien to society. To see life in this way is to see love as a self-creating relation hovering over what denies it and can never be fully expressed in it. It is not possession of money which gives value to Bella, but her power to take the energy of her love for her father, her husband, and her child and use them as the motive power for a domestic drama which they "mutually" create for themselves.

Bella's creation of the authenticity of her own life is parallel to the structure of imaginary and real in the narrative design of the novel. The novelist's search for reality by playing the role of a narrator who exists only within an imaginary world is analogous to the game by which Bella becomes herself by playing the role of a sister or mother to her father, treating him like a cherubic child. It is therefore no accident that the marriage of Bella and John is shown through the eyes of a narrator within the narrator, a mirror within the mirror, old Gruff and Glum, a wooden-legged Greenwich pensioner who sees the marriage as a fairy-tale come true: "For years, the wings of his mind had gone to look after the legs of his body; but Bella had brought them back for him per steamer, and they were spread again. He was a slow sailer on a wind of happiness,

111

but he took a cross cut for the rendezvous, and pegged away as if he were scoring furiously at cribbage. . . . And long on the bright steps stood Gruff and Glum, looking after the pretty bride, with a narcotic consciousness of having dreamed a dream" (IV. 4. 751–752).

As in the case of the Analytical, Gruff and Glum's name is a product of linguistic substitutions. He lives as the adjectives which describe him. His nautical past has so pervaded his life that he sees everything according to maritime metaphors. These transform the scene around him into a dream matching his nature. His dream exists within the dream world of the novel to generate another example of that interplay of imaginary and real I have called the Quaker Oats box effect. Such an interplay is especially appropriate here because it matches so exactly the nature of what Gruff and Glum witnesses. Having gone through a kind of death, Bella and John are liberated from the coercive power of the Harmon will. They are now paradoxically free to carry out its terms in an assumption of roles sustained only by their spontaneous love for one another. The passage quoted above brings together three forms of the same structure: the doubling of metaphor in the heavily figurative texture of the language, the doubling of narrator within narrator, and the doubling of the narrator's power to transform reality in the protagonists' ability to change their lives by living them according to the patterns of the imagination. Here as in other Victorian novels society is

seen not as founded on some sustaining reality outside itself, but as created by people in their living
together. It is therefore not different in structure or
substance from the novel which reflects it.

4

George Eliot, as many critics have seen, is the
most explicit example of the Victorian transformation from a view of society as based on a transcendent ground to a view of it as generating itself. When
Marian Evans became George Eliot she did so by
assuming the personality of a Feuerbachian general
consciousness, the mind not of a specific society but
of all humanity. Her narrator is also able, as I have
said, to speak for the mind of a local community
and for the individual sensibility. The sympathetic
participation of the narrator in the subtle move-
ments of thought in the individual character takes
place within a consciousness as wide as all mankind,
and this justifies the narrator in claiming he has the
angelic omniscience of "Uriel watching the progress
of planetary history from the Sun."[5] The narrator
can move at will in time and space anywhere within
his encompassing mind, making connections, com-
parisons, juxtapositions, and generalizations on the
basis of a universal knowledge. George Eliot's
novels follow individual destinies within the context of an inclusive wisdom.

Dorothea Brooke, in *Middlemarch,* is one of the
most important of such characters. Like Henry

Esmond, like Ayala in Trollope's *Ayala's Angel*, like Eustacia Vye in *The Return of the Native,* and like many other heroes and heroines of Victorian novels, Dorothea has needs which are described in specifically religious terms. She seeks a divine power which will transfigure her life, give her concrete duties and tasks, and at the same time ratify these in terms of absolute sanctions. Like St. Theresa she is someone whose flamelike spirit, "fed from within, soared after some illimitable satisfaction, some object which would never justify weariness, which would reconcile self-despair with the rapturous consciousness of life beyond self" (I. "Prelude." 2). Dorothea wants to "cast herself, with a childlike sense of reclining, in the lap of a divine consciousness which sustain[s] her own" (I. 5. 62). Her mind is "theoretic, and yearn[s] by its nature after some lofty conception of the world which might frankly include the parish of Tipton and her own rule of conduct there" (I. 1. 9). She is "enamoured of intensity and greatness, and rash in embracing whatever seem[s] to her to have those aspects" (I. 1.9). She seeks above all a "submergence of self in communion with Divine perfection" (I. 3. 34).

If such a need could only be satisfied by a god, the dramatic action of Dorothea's part of the novel follows from the fact that she seeks satisfaction of her desire in a relation to another human being who will be as a god to her. Her love for Casaubon is defined in just these terms. When he explains his mythological theories to her he is, as the narrator

114

says, like Milton's "affable archangel" instructing
Eve, and to her he seems "a living Bossuet," "a
modern Augustine who unite[s] the glories of doc-
tor and saint" (I. 3. 32–34). He is like Oberlin,
like a reincarnation of his seventeenth century
namesake, like St. Thomas Aquinas. "Everyday-
things," thinks Dorothea, "with us would mean the
greatest things. It would be like marrying Pascal"
(I. 3. 40). Her love for Casaubon, the narrator
explains, is a transference of her religious yearnings
to her future husband and is based on the assumption that he can incarnate for her that absolute justification for her daily acts which she demands: "The
intensity of her religious disposition, the coercion
it exercised over her life, was but one aspect of a
nature altogether ardent, theoretic, and intellectually
consequent . . . . The thing which seemed to her
best, she wanted to justify by the completest knowledge . . . . Into this soul-hunger as yet all her youthful passion was poured; the union which attracted
her was one that would deliver her from her girl-
ish subjection to her own ignorance, and give her
the freedom of voluntary submission to a guide
who would take her along the grandest path" (I.
3. 39–40).

Dorothea's marriage to Casaubon leads to her
discovery that no man can be a god for another in a
world without God. As in the case of similar dis-
coveries made by Henry Esmond or by Eustacia
Vye, this revelation has two aspects. Both are versions of the discovery that each man is the center

115

of his own world and makes his own subjective interpretation of it. Each man casts outward on the world patterns of value which have no existence except in his own mind.

Dorothea's interpretation of Casaubon has been a fantasy of her mind, the projection of notions which shape the small knowledge she has of Casaubon according to her private patterns of desire. Though it takes Dorothea many painful months of marriage to discover this, the narrator knows it from the beginning and lets the reader know. "[H]e thinks a whole world of which my thought is but a poor twopenny mirror," says Dorothea to herself of her lover. "And his feelings too, his whole experience—what a lake compared with my little pool!" Upon which the narrator comments with that remorseless clairvoyance which characterizes his insight throughout: "Miss Brooke argued from words and dispositions not less unhesitatingly than other young ladies of her age. Signs are small measurable things, but interpretations are illimitable, and in girls of sweet, ardent nature, every sign is apt to conjure up wonder, hope, belief, vast as a sky, and coloured by a diffused thimbleful of matter in the shape of knowledge" (I. 3. 34). The "radiance of [Dorothea's] transfigured girlhood [has fallen] on the first object that [has come] within its level" (I. 5. 63), and Casaubon has been "the mere occasion which [has] set alight the fine inflammable material of her youthful illusions" (I. 10. 124).

The reason why Casaubon cannot stand in the

116

place of God for Dorothea is another version of
George Eliot's commitment to the idea that each
man is imprisoned in himself. No man can be a god
for another because each man is no more than one
subjective interpretation of the world, never an
absolute perspective on it like that which the narrator possesses by virtue of his identification with
the mind of mankind. George Eliot differs from
other Victorian novelists in the consistency of her
commitment to this form of subjectivism. The characters in Trollope's novels, for example, attain in
the end a more or less complete identification with
the collective wisdom of the community. In their
assent to its habits and judgments they come to see
things as the narrator sees them. Dickens' characters
too approach a wisdom like that of the narrator, and
the climax of Hardy's best novels is a moment in
which the protagonist, Henchard, Tess, Eustacia, or
Jude, achieves something like the detached vision
of the futility of life which the narrator has had all
along. George Eliot's characters, on the other hand,
even the intelligent and sensitive ones like Dorothea,
never fully attain the narrator's vision. Though
Dorothea escapes from her false dreams and from
her self-pity to share in the ongoing march of mankind, the narrator still has to speak for her in the
last pages of the novel. He defines the meaning of
her life in a way Dorothea herself would not quite
be able to do it. Every man, however self-denying
and sympathetic he may be, still remains a "centre
of self, whence the lights and shadows must always

117

fall with a certain difference" (I. 21. 323). This is the point of the beautiful "parable" of the pier-glass which is "minutely and multitudinously scratched in all directions." These scratches appear to arrange themselves in a fine series of concentric circles if a candle is approached to the glass. "The scratches are events, and the candle is the egoism of any person . . ." (I. 27. 403).

It might appear that this is the culmination of George Eliot's vision: an irreconcilable contradiction between the subjective distortion of reality by the individual and the narrator's transindividual vision of the whole truth. Each center of experience, however, is not altogether isolated. It is a node in a network of relations which ultimately includes all of society. The image of a network or web pervades *Middlemarch,* as Reva Stump has shown.[6] "I at least," says the narrator, "have so much to do in unravelling certain human lots, and seeing how they were woven and interwoven, that all the light I can command must be concentrated on this particular web . . ." (I. 15. 214). According to the narrator's vision, the society of *Middlemarch* is an immensely complicated moving network of relationships which includes many different levels of "minutiae" in its interaction, the "minutiæ of mental make in which one of us differs from another" (I. 15. 226), the "subtle . . . process of . . . gradual change" in the individual (I. 15. 219), the complex of "details and relations" (I. 16. 248) in the interplay between one mind and another, and, outside these, the "frustrating complexity" (I. 18. 274) of social conditions. In the narrator's vision men can be seen to "have numerous strands of experience lying side by side and never compare them with each other" (III. 58. 84), but no human fact exists in isolation from the others. It is tied to them both within one individual and in relation to other men, as each thread in a cloth is interwoven with the others. Each person at any moment of his life is a special perspective on his whole life and on the life of the community, like the candle which is a "little sun" organizing all the scratches on the glass into concentric circles. No man is isolated from his fellows, but is always "moving with kindred natures in the same embroiled medium, the same troublous fitfully-illuminated life" (II. 30. 27). Every act of a man has an incalculably diffusive effect on that tangled whole.

The Victorian novelists, Dickens, Thackeray, or Trollope as well as George Eliot, are unwilling to accept the notion so prevalent in fiction after Conrad and James, that no comprehensive vision of society is possible. Dickens, for example, writes in a memorandum book kept at about the time he was planning *Our Mutual Friend* of a story "representing London—or Paris, or any other great place— in the light of being actually unknown to all the people in the story, and only taking the colour of their fears and fancies and opinions. So getting a new aspect, and being unlike itself. An *odd* unlikeness of itself."[8] Each city-dweller sees the city

119

according to his own perspective on it, and in his eyes it becomes something strangely unlike itself, a subjective fantasy. The narrator of *Our Mutual Friend,* however, sees the city and its citizens as they really are. Just as the River Thames winds through *Our Mutual Friend* as it winds through London, joining the diverse milieux of the novel and symbolically expressing the unity of the community, so the narrator is a pervasive consciousness viewing each man in terms of his relations to his fellows. These ramifying interconnections bind each character to all the others, and make the novel a model in miniature of the whole of London in its unimaginable complexity. In the same way the provincial society of Middlemarch is a synecdoche for larger social structures, for urban society, or for all English society—the small standing for the large, the simple for the complex, in a version of pastoral which makes *Middlemarch,* like *Our Mutual Friend, Vanity Fair,* or *The Way We Live Now,* a representation of the structure of relationships within a whole culture. In this it is like those early sociological models which George Eliot's associate Herbert Spencer and others were developing during the Victorian period.

Dorothea's deepest insight into the way she is woven into the fabric of mankind comes when she has spent her night of suffering after the false revelation of Will Ladislaw's betrayal of her. In the early morning she looks out of her window (the motif recurs in the novel), and sees "a man with a bundle on his back and a woman carrying her baby," figures moving in a field, and feels "the largeness of the world and the manifold wakings of men to labour and endurance." She recognizes then that she is "a part of that involuntary, palpitating life, and [can] neither look out on it from her luxurious shelter as a mere spectator, nor hide her eyes in selfish complaining" (III. 80. 392). This insight sends her to offer her sympathizing love to Rosamond, and it leads her soon after to give up the money which was the basis of her abstract plans to do good in the community. She gives up her fortune in order to accept a narrow role as the wife of Will Ladislaw, rising politician and "ardent public man" (III. "Finale." 461). She is "absorbed into the life of another," and, far from attaining an illimitable satisfaction, is "only known in a certain circle as a wife and mother" (ibid.).

The narrator provides the ultimate wisdom which is to be drawn from her experience and speaks for that understanding which the individual can never fully attain. No divinely justified role in life is possible, the narrator sees, no place in society which is at once universal and concrete, no discovery of another person who can stand in place of God, no attainment of angelic breadth of vision and action for oneself. Each person, however, is part of the embroiled medium of the whole community, and though he may not rise upward like a flame toward a limitless joy dependent on some preexisting divine absolute, he may in "self-subduing act[s] of fellowship," acts which have a "divine efficacy of rescue"

121

(III. 82. 414), dissolve into the community, like a river dispersing in the sand, so joining the "choir invisible" made up of all the quiet acts of sympathy of men and women living together. In this way he will do his part toward the creation of the collective mind of humanity which is for George Eliot the God men make for themselves in their living together. "Souls," as she says, "live on in perpetual echoes" (I. 16. 243), and in that living on bring God into existence, for "God . . . manifest[s] himself by our silent feeling, and make[s] his love felt through ours,"[9] or, as Feuerbach puts it, "Man with man—the unity of I and Thou—is God."[10] "Her finely-touched spirit had still its fine issues, though they were not widely visible," says the narrator in the beautiful sentences which end *Middlemarch* and view Dorothea's life in the context of the whole life of mankind. "Her full nature, like that river of which Cyrus broke the strength, spent itself in channels which had no great name on the earth. But the effect of her being on those around her was incalculably diffusive: for the growing good of the world is partly dependent on unhistoric acts; and that things are not so ill with you and me as they might have been, is half owing to the number who lived faithfully a hidden life, and rest in unvisited tombs" (III. "Finale." 465).[11] The reader is here invited to join with his fellows and to think of himself as part of the community of mankind for which the narrator speaks. We are part of the community which has been ameliorated by Dorothea's unhistoric acts of love. Such is George Eliot's version of the notion, so widespread in Victorian fiction, that society is generated and sustained by individual acts of self-denying, self-creating love.

5

Like George Eliot's fiction, Trollope's novels reveal the covert structure of society by the indirect means of exploring individual quests for self-fulfillment. His fiction concentrates with admirable consistency on the question of what constitutes authentic selfhood. Each novel is a variation on this theme and brings another aspect of it to light. If the narrator is a genial giant who has hewn out a solid piece of English earth and speaks as the collective mind of the community, much of the texture of each novel is made up of passages in which the narrator enters into the mind of one member of this community and represents with perfect tact each nuance of his thought.

For Trollope no individual can fulfill himself in isolation. A man comes into existence in his relations to other people. The person and his social role are identical. This role, however, is not given with birth. It does not coincide with the person's inherited place in a family or in a social class. It is created only in the fundamental decisions of the self. These are made in the context of the initially given place in society, but may change the character's relation to that context. In any case they determine more exactly that relation, place the character once and for all as involved in a certain way in the community.

For Trollope the most important example of this commitment of the self is falling in love. Almost any of Trollope's novels would provide an example of this theme, but a late novel, *Ayala's Angel,* is one of the subtlest as well as one of the most characteristically Trollopean in the beguiling willfulness of its heroine and in the attractive tang of irony, so typical of Trollope, which lies in the discrepancy between the heroine's uncertainty about her future and the reader's certainty, guided by the narrator's equanimity, that all will end happily.

At the center of this novel, as of so many others by Trollope, is the idea that a man's substance is his love for another person. I am my love for the other. My selfhood is outside myself and can move from possibility to actuality only when my love is returned. It must be embodied in marriage and in assimilation into the community's structure of roles and relationships. My falling in love is not, however, governed by the collective wisdom of society. A man cannot choose to love or not to love someone, nor can any other person or group exert the least effective pressure to determine authentic loving. Falling in love is a spontaneous commitment of one self to another, a commitment in which the person comes into existence as himself once and for all.

Falling in love is for Trollope an absolute. It cannot be explained in terms of any cause or ground which precedes it and which supports it in existence —neither the personality of the lover, nor the personality of the loved one, nor any social criteria of choice, nor any divine impetus which says I can become myself by loving such and such a person. Falling in love is uncaused and unfounded, a gratuitous flowing out of the self toward another person. Moreover, the man or woman who falls in love gives himself entirely to the person he loves, as in *Dr. Wortle's School* (1881), Mrs. Peacocke describes the moment when, without needing to speak at all, she gave herself forever to the man who became her husband: "He had never said a word. He tried not to look it. But I knew that I had his heart and that he had mine. From that moment I have thought of him day and night. When I gave him my hand then as he parted from me, I gave it him as his own. It has been his to do what he liked with it ever since, let who might live or who might die."[12]

Trollope often emphasizes what is spontaneous, irrational, and uncontrollable about falling in love. In *Ayala's Angel,* for example, Ayala asks: "How can I help it? One does not fall in love by trying,— nor by trying prevent it,"[13] or in *An Old Man's Love,* published posthumously in 1884, the heroine, Mary Lawrie, is unable to love Mr. Whittlestaff however hard she tries, and unable not to love John Gordon:

"But I accepted you;" [she says to Mr. Whittlestaff,] "and I determined to love you with all my heart,—

125

with all my heart."

"And," [he replies,] "you knew that you would love him without any determination. . . . No; you cannot love two men. You would have tried to love me and have failed. You would have tried not to love him, and have failed then also."[14]

Trollope's characters do not justify their loving in any rational or theoretical terms. They speak rather with a wholesome vagueness about having a "sort of feeling" that they love someone. They are unwilling to seek reasons for this feeling, to uncover its grounds, or to clarify it. To clarify it would be to falsify it, for it is no more than a feeling. When the characters delay in committing themselves to another person, this is not so that they can make up their minds, but in order to allow their spontaneous feelings to become manifest. Such a commitment of the self cannot be hurried by taking thought, and a decision which is made on abstract grounds or on grounds of social prudence is shallow and insubstantial. Once Trollope's characters have become aware of the direction in which their feeling has moved, they become extraordinarily tenacious in sticking to this commitment against all opposition or difficulty, even when sticking to it is most disadvantageous from a worldly point of view. They hold to it because it is what they are. It is all they have, as Adelaide Palliser, in *Phineas Redux,* explains in justification of her love for Gerard Maule:

"You ask me why I got into his boat," [she says to Lady Chiltern.] "Why does any girl get into a man's

126

boat? Why did you get into Lord Chiltern's?"

"I promised to marry him when I was seven years old;—so he says."

"But you wouldn't have done it, if you hadn't had a sort of feeling that you were born to be his wife. I haven't got into this man's boat yet; but I never can be happy unless I do, simply because—"

"You love him."

"Yes;—just that. I have a feeling that I should like to be in his boat, and I shouldn't like to be anywhere else. After you have come to feel like that about a man I don't suppose it makes any difference whether you think him perfect or imperfect. He's just my own,—at least I hope so;—the one thing that I've got. If I wear a stuff frock, I'm not going to despise it because it's not silk." (41. II. 7)

Being in love is as substantial a fact as having one garment rather than another. But though it is not in control of conscious choosing, it is nonetheless an act of the will. For Trollope the self is an energy of volition which is the focusing of the whole self on another person. Eventually Trollope's good characters become aware that their spontaneous wills have chosen for them, that they now exist as a force of loving so fundamental to them that they cannot betray their love without betraying themselves. The good characters then ratify their involuntary wills with an act of voluntary willing which puts the rational and irrational levels of the self in harmony. Such a choice is usually in conflict with the obvious social good of the lover. All his friends, family, and the community generally advise him to do otherwise than he does, as, for example, in

127

Mr. Scarborough's Family everyone tells Florence Mountjoy to give up Harry Annesley. Usually, as in this case, the issue is money. The lovers will not have enough income to live in a way proper for ladies and gentlemen in English society. This conflict between self-fulfillment and social obligation recurs again and again in Trollope's fiction. While the conflict persists there is an incompatibility between the commitment of the self in loving and the absorption of the person into the community of ladies and gentlemen. At the same time, however, Trollope sees clearly that a person cannot fulfill himself in isolation either from the one individual he loves or from society as a whole. The lover's problem is to get his love made real in its acceptance by the loved one and by the community. Until this happens he is incomplete.

The character who gives her name to *Ayala's Angel* is an admirable example of this. Ayala's "Angel" is her subjective image of the man who will be worthy of her love. He will be an "Angel of Light," divine in his beauty and in his superiority to ordinary mankind. "If there was any law of right and wrong fixed absolutely in her bosom, it was this,—that no question of happiness or unhappiness, of suffering or joy, would affect her duty to the Angel of Light. She owed herself to him should he come to seek her. She owed herself to him no less, even should he fail to come. And she owed herself equally whether he should be rich or poor" (26. 242). Measuring the men who propose marriage to her by this theoretical model, she obstinately refuses them one by one, rejecting firmly the counsels of her uncles and aunts, her friends, and the collective judgment of society, saying to each suitor, by her refusal rather than by her words, for she keeps her image of the Angel a jealous secret hidden in her heart: "You are not he,—not he, not that Angel of Light, which must come to me, radiant with poetry, beautiful to the eye, full of all excellences of art, lifted above the earth by the qualities of his mind, —such a one as must come to me if it be that I am ever to confess that I love. You are not he, and I cannot love you" (25. 238).

Ayala's obstinacy is a defense of her selfhood from the pressures of the community. To accept someone she does not love would be to deny herself any authenticity as a person. The narrator therefore fully approves of her stubbornness. It is, like the stubbornness of so many of Trollope's girls, the doubling of the first involuntary will by a second voluntary choice, the will as free decision ratifying the will as spontaneous power of loving. Or rather, it is a negative version of this theme. As long as Ayala is not conscious of having fallen in love she is right to refuse all offers for her hand. "How is a girl to love a man if she does not love him?" she asks (27. 259). At the same time, however, the narrator deplores Ayala's isolation from the community. This isolation is defined by the fact that she does not tell anyone of her secret expectation that an Angel of Light will appear to love her. Such an iso-

129

lation is commitment to a romantic invention. It is a kind of insanity. A subjective idea not embodied in relationships to others is always dangerously akin to madness for Trollope, as, for example, in the central story of Louis Trevelyan in *He Knew He Was Right* (1868–1869), or in the parallel story of Robert Kennedy in *Phineas Redux*. As long as Ayala has not found a real man who incarnates the qualities she has imagined for her angel she is in a dangerous state of solitude and incompleteness, for all her beauty and charm. In the same way, poor Tom Tringle, hopelessly in love with Ayala, will end in the insane asylum, as his father foresees, if he remains the prisoner of a love which cannot ever be fulfilled.

Here the subplots of *Ayala's Angel,* according to a paralleling usual in Trollope's fiction, are analogous to the main plot and act as a commentary on it. Ayala's sister Lucy commits herself wholly to her lover, Isadore Hamel. Like Mrs. Peacocke in *Dr. Wortle's School,* she says she belongs to her lover and will do whatever he says. Lucy serves as an example of authentic love against which Ayala's prolonged failure to know that she is in love may be measured. The relationship of Frank Houston and Imogene Docimer is another kind of commentary on the main story. It is a good demonstration of the way Trollope's lovers, like Johnny Eames in *The Last Chronicle of Barset,* or Frank Greystock in *The Eustace Diamonds* (1873), or Lady Laura Kennedy in *Phineas Redux,* may choose wilfully to betray their love for another person without permanently damaging the integrity of their identities. It is not in their power to cease loving, but it is in their power to act in ways which temporarily or even permanently deny that love fulfillment. Since Frank Houston thinks he does not have money enough to marry Imogene honorably, he attempts to make a cynical marriage for money to Gertrude Tringle. When he escapes from this entanglement and comes back to Imogene in spite of his poverty, he can say truthfully that this is no renewal of his affections. It is an act of voluntary willing at last in accord with the orientation his spontaneous will has maintained all along: "It is no return," he says. "There has never been a moment in which my affections have not been the same" (41. 398).

In the same way, when Ayala finally comes to accept Jonathan Stubbs, after a series of gradual approaches toward a recognition that she loves him, Trollope has her reiterate her knowledge that she has loved him from the instant she first met him. "I think I fell in love with him the first moment I saw him," she says at last (55. 538). It was love at first sight, that fundamental allegiance of the whole substance of the self in an outward movement of the involuntary will which constitutes true selfhood for Trollope. Ayala is for a long time, however, unaware of what has happened to her. Her abstract fidelity to the idea that an Angel of Light will come to her keeps her from understanding herself and

131

leads her to refuse Jonathan Stubbs's proposals repeatedly. The central sequence of the novel focuses not on her gradual change, for she does not change, but on her gradual discovery of who she is. Her obstinate allegiance to what Trollope calls "the theory of her life" (49. 474) keeps her from being immediately transparent to herself. The same phrase had been used to describe Frank Houston's decision not to marry Imogene. "The whole theory of his life," says the narrator when Frank returns to Imogene, "had,—with a vengeance,—been thrown to the winds" (41.398). Ayala can finally bring theory and spontaneous feeling into harmony when she discovers that Jonathan Stubbs is in fact that Angel of Light for whom she has longed:

> It was of him she had always dreamed even long before she had seen him. He was the man, perfect in all good things, who was to come and take her with him;—if ever man should come and take her. . . . In the fulness of her dreams there had never been more than the conviction that such a being, and none other, could be worthy of her love. There had never been faith in the hope that such a one would come to her, —never even though she would tell herself that angels had come down from heaven and had sought in marriage the hands of the daughters of men. Her dreams had been to her a barrier against love rather than an encouragement. But now he that she had in truth dreamed of had come for her. (52.506; 55.539–540)

The way in which interpersonal relations replace religious experience for Trollope is particularly clear in this text, with its explicit echo of Genesis 6:2:

". . . the sons of God saw the daughters of men that they were fair; and they took them wives of all which they chose." Ayala's Angel of Light is a specifically religious concept, the idea of a superhuman figure who will transform her life by loving her and on whom her self-fulfillment depends as that of a Christian does on being chosen by God. She discovers finally that the part of herself which is outside herself, the ground of her selfhood, is Jonathan Stubbs: ". . . he was in truth the very 'Angel of Light'" (55. 540). Until she finds a real person to embody the subjective image she has cherished within her imagination, she remains only an insubstantial image of unfulfilled desire, but such a person does come to her. Trollope's novels, unlike those of Hardy, can end happily because one person can, for Trollope, stand in the place of God to another and be the foundation and support of his selfhood.

If the self, for Trollope, affirms itself in terms of the other, this means that the willing reiteration of the deepest involuntary energy of the self is the origin of society. Society is constantly renewed in acts of self-affirmation which sustain the community and keep it from becoming an empty framework of conventions, habits, rules, judgments, and institutions. Trollope's view of society is like those cosmological theories which suppose the continuous creation of matter and energy. According to such theories, new matter and energy are constantly flowing in from some ubiquitous creative source, perhaps at innu-

133

merable points in the universe. So for Trollope, each duplication of spontaneous choice by voluntary choice, a choice often made in denial of the particular role in the community the individual has inherited, sustains the community and is its source.

In *Dr. Wortle's School*, for example, it is right that Mr. and Mrs. Peacocke should continue to live together as man and wife, even though they discover that they are not married in the eyes of the law. She has become bone of his bone and flesh of his flesh. This extra-social union is more important than the abstract convention of marriage. Marriage as an institution within the community has its source and validity in the unsponsored commitments of one person to another. The marriage bond is descriptive rather than prescriptive. Authentic relations between persons are self-creating.

The fundamental revelation of Trollope's novels is the dependence of the general mind on particular minds. The collective mind exists only in individuals as they are related to one another. It is generated only by them and sustained only by them. The narrator, who speaks for the general mind, has therefore been brought into existence by the characters, so that it may be said that the narrator is made by his world rather than that he makes the world of the story he tells. He has risen magically into being out of the interchanges between person and person and is kept in being only so long as those interchanges continue.

The collective consciousness is like each individual consciousness in that it exists as the spontaneous will to sustain itself as continuous with itself. Like the individual self, it is sustained by nothing outside mankind. It is for this reason that Trollope puts such a high value on the unbroken historical continuity of English society, and, like Walter Bagehot, whom he much resembles in sensibility and in outlook,[15] has such distaste for sudden changes in society and such faith in open discussion among gentlemen and ladies as capable of maintaining the unbroken flow of the community through time. The fact that a culture is a collective game, the shared will to go on living by certain rules of action and judgment, is not seen by those living within the culture and accepting its rules as absolutely valid. The action of a novel by Trollope is a temporary whirlpool in the midst of the surrounding mind of the community. This local disturbance reveals the fact that society is a structure which organizes itself according to its own immanent laws and without the intervention of any superhuman lawgiving power.

In *Ayala's Angel,* as in most of Trollope's novels, the whirlpool in the end vanishes, the characters fulfill themselves and melt into the collective mind for which the older characters, happily settled into a place in society, have spoken throughout the story. During the prolonged period of uncertainty which takes up most of the novel, however, this coincidence of private self and social self is for the protagonists held open as unfulfilled possibility. The main characters, Ayala, Lucy, Tom Tringle, Frank Houston,

Imogene Docimer, still exist as unassuaged desire. Their continuation in this state reveals the fact that society transcends its individuals and yet exists only in terms of its individuals, as a game transcends its players, but exists only in the individual actions of each player. The player brings something irreplaceable to the game, his strength of willing, and yet he exists only in terms of his relations to others. By choosing a story which puts the game in question, *Ayala's Angel,* like *Henry Esmond, Our Mutual Friend,* or *Middlemarch,* allows the reader to glimpse during the time before it closes in on itself, the secret presence which sustains the whole. This presence disappears if one tries to fix it in a single person. It exists only in the intercourse between persons. In the same way, the source of meaning which makes language possible can be located in no single word, but only in the interaction of words in syntactical patterns. The power of structures of words to create meaning is usually taken for granted. It becomes visible in language turned back on itself, for example, in poetry. The novel, to follow out this analogy, might be defined as the poetry of interpersonal relations.

Victorian fiction raises for the twentieth-century reader the dark question of whether the assimilation of the protagonists into the community by way of a happy relation to another person is a valid resolution, or whether, to our deeper insight, it should appear as a covering over and forgetting of the fundamental fact of human existence so persuasively dramatized in the body of the book—in the desire for some "illimitable satisfaction" of Dorothea in *Middlemarch,* for example, or in Ayala's grandiose dreams in *Ayala's Angel.* This is the question, to continue my analogy between language and interpersonal relations, of whether the perfected sentence brings into the open the latent principle of meaning which makes language possible, or whether it hides it. Perhaps the power behind language is only brought to the surface in the gaps between words, in the failures of language, not in its completed articulations. Correspondingly, human beings, it may be, are characterized by unappeasable desire and consequently by permanent alienation from their deepest selves. Any replacement of desire by fulfillment is only temporary and illusory. For the Victorian novelists, on the other hand, the existence of an authentic satisfaction of desire makes the happy ending possible, though by no means inevitable.

In Trollope's case, for example, the happy ending is reached in spite of many opportunities for failure. Along with those characters like Ayala who obtain a final happiness, there are those, like Lily Dale in *The Small House at Allington* and *The Last Chronicle of Barset,* who remain in unfulfillment, or those, like Johnny Eames in the same novels or Lady Laura Kennedy in *Phineas Redux,* who commit themselves in love to another person, but never, for one reason or another, attain possession of that person, or those, like Louis Trevelyan in *He Knew He Was Right* or Robert Kennedy in *Phineas Redux,* whose conscious wills have in some strange way lost contact with their spontaneous wills. The obstinacy of such characters gradually so alienates them from themselves that they are led step by step to destroy their own lives. Nevertheless, most of Trollope's novels end for the main characters in a happy coincidence of private self and social role.

Hardy's difference, perhaps his "modernity," lies in the fact that the desire of his protagonists— Eustacia, Henchard, or Jude—remains illimitable, and so his most characteristic novels must end unhappily. Whenever Hardy's characters attain what have seemed their goals, their longings are magically constituted anew and reoriented toward something or someone they do not yet possess. In Trollope's fiction, on the contrary, the angelic ideal may be incarnated in another person, and possession of that person brings peace. Even so, Trollope has a strong sense that the life of the individual and of the community is a continuing process. A certain openness to new involvements remains even in those who appear to be most settled into a role in society and to have obtained the fixed self which accompanies it. The most obvious evidence of the open-endedness of Trollope's novels is the persistence of the same characters from novel to novel as persons who may still have new experiences involving the deepest reality of the self. Examples of characters who appear in this way in more than one novel are Septimus Harding, Mrs. Proudie, Lily Dale, Lady Glencora, and Phineas Finn. For Trollope, each man or women depends on others, who depend in turn on others, in an endless round of encounters forming a constant interplay of wills. The process of mutual dependence suggests covertly, however, that there is a hidden foundation within the social game. This foundation is revealed by Trollope's work in one of its most important manifestations: the power of willing which is intrinsic to each man and woman. The individual will, for Trollope, is the ground of everything else in society.

6

Such a self-creating system can be detected in one form or another in the work of other Victorian novelists too, as I have tried to show for Thackeray, Dickens, and George Eliot. A system of this sort is present in the time structure of Victorian fiction, in its play of imaginary and real, and in the pattern of interacting minds which generates its form.

The work of each Victorian novelist is unique. Nevertheless, a common dialectic of development may be identified in six of the most important novelists. This proceeds from the isolated mind of the author to the collective mind of a narrator who exists behind the mirror, in a realm imitating in words the social and physical reality of Victorian England. This narrator, in his turn, exploits his power to play the roles of persons who exist bathed in the surrounding medium of the general mind. By means of this double displacement, displacement into

the mirroring general consciousness and deplace-
ment into the minds of the protagonists, many characteristic Victorian novels show that society no
longer seems to have a transcendent origin and support. This leads in turn to the discovery that the individual human heart generates the game of society
and establishes its rules. Society rests on human feeling and on human will. It is created by the interplay of one mind and heart with another.

All this is shown within the looking-glass world
of fiction. The play of reality within reality in a
novel, of narrator within narrator, of language
within language, leads ultimately, however, to the
revelation that both sides of the looking glass are
the same. Human culture and the imitation of human culture in a novel have the same substance and
the same structure. Both have the nature of language. What is true within the looking-glass world
of the novel is also true in reality. Many Victorian
novels suggest that man on this side of the mirror
too lives his life in relations to his fellows which
are like the transformations of metaphor. These exchanges reveal in their juxtapositions of sameness
and difference the immanent power which is the
hidden center of what seems centerless, the source
and ground of what seems to have neither source nor
ground.

1. *A Portrait of the Artist as a Young Man* (New York, 1956), Ch. 5, p. 214.

2. See "Anthony Trollope," *The Art of Fiction and Other Essays* (New York: Oxford University Press, 1948), pp. 65–66.

3. *Satires,* I, 1, 69–70.

4. Perhaps the best example of this is the chapter describing the clandestine excursion to Greenwich of Bella and her father (Bk. II, Ch. 8, "In Which an Innocent Elopement Occurs"). See especially pp. 358–359.

5. *Middlemarch,* ed. cit., II, Ch. 41, p. 211.

6. In *Movement and Vision in George Eliot's Novels* (Seattle: University of Washington Press, 1959).

7. See Footnote 41 of Chapter Three for examples of the motif of "minutiae."

8. *Letters,* ed. Walter Dexter, The Nonesuch Edition, III (Bloomsbury: The Nonesuch Press, 1938), 788.

9. *Adam Bede,* ed. cit., II, Ch. 45, p. 242.

10. *The Essence of Christianity,* ed. cit., p. xiii.

11. Gordon S. Haight, in the Riverside Edition of *Middlemarch* (Boston, 1956), pp. 612–613, calls attention to changes from the first edition in the final version of the last paragraphs of the novel.

12. The World's Classics edition (London, 1960), Part V, Ch. 7, pp. 208–209.

13. The World's Classics edition (London, 1960), Ch. 43, p. 417.

14. The World's Classics edition (London, 1936), Ch. 23, p. 249.

15. For a discussion of some aspects of this relationship see Asa Briggs, "Trollope, Bagehot, and the English Constitution," *Victorian People: A Reassessment of Persons and Themes, 1851–1867,* Harper Colophon Books (New York and Evanston: Harper & Row, 1963), pp. 87–115.

INDEX

The novel in which a character or place appears is given in parentheses after the name. Novels mentioned frequently in the Index are abbreviated according to the following code: *Oliver Twist:* OT; *Our Mutual Friend:* OMF; *Adam Bede:* AB; *Middlemarch:* M; *A Pair of Blue Eyes:* PBE; *Henry Esmond:* HE; *Vanity Fair:* VF; *Ayala's Angel:* AA; *The Last Chronicle of Barset:* LCB; *Phineas Redux:* PR.

Index

Index

Index

Index